WALK DERBY

G000098473

30 Circular Walks
with detailed instructions
and maps

CONTRIBUTORS

Frank Rodgers has provided 16 of these walks. Other contributors are Norman Anderson; Norman Sanders; Albert Weatherley; Tony Beardsley and Maurice Wall.

Maps by PAUL WILLIAMSON

Ninth and completely revised edition

DERBYSHIRE COUNTRYSIDE LTD
Lodge Lane, Derby

ISBN 0 85100 091 6

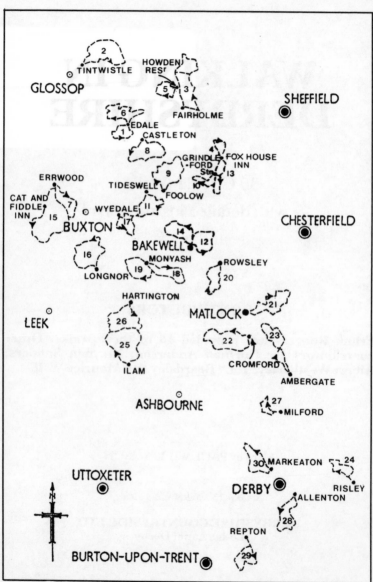

GLOSSOP

SHEFFIELD

2 TINTWISTLE
HOWDEN RES?
5 3
6 FAIRHOLME
EDALE
1 CASTLETON
8 GRINDLE-FORD FOX HOUSE INN
Stn. 13
9 10
ERRWOOD TIDESWELL FOOLOW
CAT AND FIDDLE INN 7 WYEDALE 11 CHESTERFIELD
15 17
BUXTON 14
BAKEWELL 12
16 MONYASH ROWSLEY
LONGNOR 19 18 20

HARTINGTON MATLOCK
LEEK 26 21
25 22 23
ILAM CROMFORD
AMBERGATE
ASHBOURNE
27
MILFORD

30 MARKEATON 24
UTTOXETER RISLEY
DERBY ALLENTON
28
REPTON
29
BURTON-UPON-TRENT

2

ROUTES

PREFACE

This ninth edition has been completely revised and all the walks have been personally checked by the contributors.

Derbyshire is a very beautiful county and those who are not familiar with it are respectfully reminded of the Country Code:

Guard against all risk of fire.

Fasten all gates.

Keep dogs under proper control.

Keep to the paths across farm land.

Avoid damaging fences, hedges and walls.

Leave no litter.

Safeguard water supplies.

Protect wild life, wild plants and trees.

Go carefully on country roads.

Respect the life of the countryside.

Vale of Edale

Go by train or car to Edale. There is a car park near the railway station. Leave the car park near the conveniences and turn right. Train passengers leave the station and turn left.

Walk beneath the railway bridge; pass the Rambler Inn and then in about 100 yards, turn left at a signpost indicating public footpath.

Go over a stile on the left, opposite a stone building. Proceed over another stile then through two fields, keeping to the tree-lined edges. On the right is steep-sided Broadleebank Tor, with the valley of the Grinds Brook beyond and Ringing Roger on the crest of the hill.

Bear slightly left across the next field, as indicated by the notice, keeping left of some farm buildings. Make for a tree with twin trunks and a sign 'path', then go over a stile.

Keep forward to a stile on the other side of a cart road. Cross the field, following the 'path' sign on a sycamore tree. On the left, the lowest part of the ridge, in between Lords Seat and Mam Tor, is Mam Nick, towards which a road winds upward.

Cross a boggy patch to a stile in a fence. Keep forward along the path with the hedge to your left and continue from stile to stile along the well-marked path, running parallel to the railway. Ahead are the rounded contours of Horsehill Tor.

Turn left over the railway bridge from which there is a fine view of the ridge culminating in the rounded cone of Lose Hill. Turn right along the road through Barber Booth, one of the five Booths in this vale. Cross the bridge over the River Noe, and by a 'one in six' gradient sign turn left along the public footpath to Castleton and Hope.

Walk east across the fields in the direction of the pointed hill (Win Hill). Behind there is a lovely view of the houses of Barber Booth nestling among the trees with the wide valley of the Noe stretching up to Edale Head.

Descend into a narrow wooded valley and cross a footbridge over a stream. Continue forward, keeping to the left of a barn, and follow the way-mark posts. Aim for a short length of wall then go ahead alongside a hedge for about 80 yards.

Follow the way-mark posts, crossing several stiles and streams until you come to a strip of woodland.

There are grand views on either side. Up the valley behind, Noe Stool stands sentinel on Edale Head; to the left is the hamlet of Grindsbrook Booth and ahead is steep Back Tor with trees along its southern slope looking like a horse's mane.

After climbing down a stile into a lane, turn right down the lane. Yet another stream crosses beneath the road. Climb gradually to Greenlands Farm. Leave the road beside the farmhouse and go over a stile, following the path to the left signposted to Castleton and Hollins Cross.

The path runs between wire fences at first until a stile and bridle gate give access to an open section. After the next stile take the middle track of the three and continue uphill to Hollins Cross. You are now at the top of the ridge and there is a fine view into the Hope Valley. Retrace your steps for about 150 yards, then take the steep path down to Hollins Farm.

Head for a stile to the left of the farm and join the farm road. Descend past another farm building to a bridge over the River Noe. Join the road by a public footpath sign and turn left. Cross Grinds Brook and the first turn right leads back to Edale Station and the Car Park. If you wish to walk into Edale village, go along the footpath indicated on the opposite side of the road.

Note: Owing to the many little mountain streams in the vicinity of some of the field paths, it is advisable to wear stout footwear when taking this walk after heavy rain.

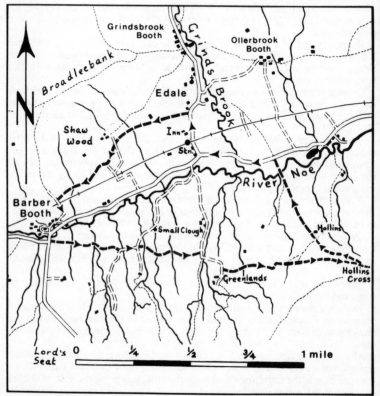

6

Tintwistle, Crowden, Chew Reservoir (Greenfield), Tintwistle

This ten-mile walk which rises to a height of 1,717 feet is based on Derbyshire's most north westerly parish, Tintwistle, but is accessible from three villages being Tintwistle and Crowden on the Woodhead Pass and Greenfield on the Oldham-Holmfirth Road. The latter walk is slightly longer and covers a distance of 14 miles.

Care must be taken on these North West Peak District Moors and one should therefore be conversant with map and compass as low cloud can strike in minutes.

The walk commences in Tintwistle in a NNW direction up Arnfield Lane behind the Church Inn and after half a mile a footpath signposted to Lad's Leap leads NE along a green boggy lane for approx. 1 mile. We then fork right to edge of moor which we cross following guide post and stakes and join footpath at entrance to a stony groove which we go up for 300 yards before following a fence to top of Tintwistle – Knarr Quarry. Here we follow guide post (to Crowden) before crossing stream to cairn and aim for tall stakes at stony bank on skyline. Follow edge round for 400 yards to deep Hollins Clough where we turn left above rocks and cross stream to guide post (Lad's Leap is on rock ledges below). Turn half right at guide post for 300 yards across moor following cairns and stakes before we bear half left along wall and along old boundary trench before beginning the steep descent along wall aiming for tall stake in wall gap.

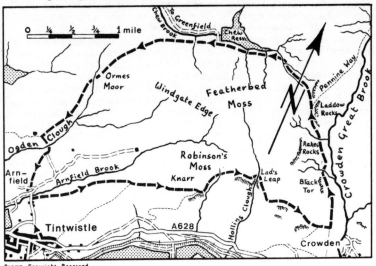

Crown Copyright Reserved

Bear half right down groove and follow wall and then through gap to Rifle Range fence which is half a mile from Crowden Youth Hostel.

Continuing our journey, follow in a northerly direction the left (West) side of iron fence until the rough path strikes higher ground, passing on its way the dripping face of Rake's Rocks. In the distance, the profile of Laddow Rocks comes into view often with the interlaced ropes of rock climbers spread across the craggy wall of the rock face. The Walker's Way, however, is not to the foot of the rocks, but to follow the steep path up the brook to the top of the outcrop and then after 250 yards swings away westwards following massive cairns until we reach Chew Reservoir.

We follow the water board track to the dam wall but instead of turning right and NW over Chew Brook and down to Greenfield (2 miles), we head WSW keeping our height and looking down on the magnificent Chew Valley.

After ¹/₂ mile we head SW over Ormes Moor before descending towards Ogden Clough and then crossing to its Western Bank our height is maintained for a further ³/₄ mile before turning sharp East and crossing the brook by a dog leg track.

We then climb a stile and head South through 3 fields before joining the farm track at Arnfield and then heading SE down Arnfield Lane to Tintwistle.

Our journey, which will have taken 4¹/₂ hours to complete, will have taken us through Derbyshire, West Yorkshire and Greater Manchester.

Route 3   **11 miles**

Derwent Edge – Howden Edge

This is a fairly tough day, combining easy valley sections with rougher high-edge walking – with spectacular views in clear weather. A pleasant cut-off is available half way round reducing the walk to about 7 miles, which will suit the less energetic. Except in mist, there are no serious navigational problems, but a compass must be carried – remember if in any trouble on the edges a compass course due west will always bring you down to the Derwent Valley. Also don't forget it will be a lot colder on the tops than it is at Fairholmes.

The start of the walk is at the Picnic Site at Fairholmes, where there is ample parking space, toilets etc. Join the road (closed to vehicles except for access) curving under the Derwent dam and follow it pleasantly along to Mill Brook. Notice, en route, The Lodge and overgrown drive of the old Derwent Hall and the few remaining houses of the drowned village of Derwent. The village itself, including the church and hall, lay down to the right, where the road swings left to cross the stream. Continue parallel to the water for a short way, but at the first gate, take the stile on the left, and climb up and across the field and up to Grindle barn. A little loss of height is involved to cross the stream, then through a gate and up the hillside quite clearly on the Jaggers' way from Cheshire to Sheffield. This old route for strings of pack animals carrying salt and other merchandise ran via Edale and Hagg Side, crossing the Derwent by the pack-horse bridge in Derwent village. The bridge would have been drowned by the Ladybower reservoir, but fortunately was taken down stone by stone and later re-erected at Slippery Stones in the Upper Derwent Valley.

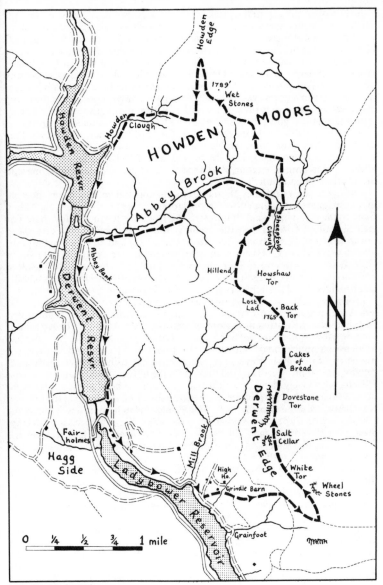

Howden Edge

1789'
Wet Stones

HOWDEN

MOORS

Howden Clough

Howden Resvr.

Abbey Brook

Sheepfold Clough

Abbey Bank

Hillend

Howshaw Tor

Derwent Resvr.

Lost Lad
1765'

Back Tor

Cakes of Bread

Dovestone Tor

Derwent Edge

Salt Cellar

Mill Brook

White Tor

Wheel Stones

Fair-holmes

Hagg Side

Ladybower Reservoir

High Ho.

Grindle Barn

Grainfoot

N

0   ¼   ½   ¾   1 mile

9

Just through the gap in the intake wall, the Jaggers route slopes to the right up the hillside, but over the past five years or so walkers – for some reason – have chosen to walk alongside the intake wall for about 300 yards and then turn left abruptly up the hillside, and this path is now clearer than the original route – a pity as the latter was superior. At the top, where the path from Ladybower crosses, turn left (north) along Derwent Edge, with splendid views all the way across the valley to Kinder, Mam Tor, and many other hills. The path is clear, though peaty in a few places. Wheel Stones (the first you come to on the right) are worth a look, as they provide a wonderful example of grit stone weathering – they also afford good shelter from a cold wind. Other interesting groups of rock lie ahead: White Tor, the Salt Cellar, Cakes of Bread and Dovestone Tor. This latter has some considerable crag below it, not usually noticed by the walker on the edge. Back Tor, the logical end of Derwent Edge, lies clearly ahead. It is an immense group of rocks and always provides shelter on one side or the other – a good lunch spot.

The deep valley of Abbey Brook lies to the north, involving a considerable loss of height. (Note, the cut-off is available here for tired walkers via Abbey Bank to the reservoir track). It is possible to head due north via Howshaw Tor into Sheepfold Clough, but the going is rough, and it is better and more rewarding to move north west from Back Tor to Lost Lad on a reasonable path. The view from Lost Lad is one of the very best in the area – pause a while. From Hillend steer north and pick up the rather faint path (to start with) leading down to the ruined cabins in the valley. These were originally shooters' cabins and provided good shelter years ago. Now, little remains except a few stones.

From the cabins, cross Sheepfold Clough, and walk round the hump on your left. A path goes ahead up to the hillside, but proceed through the gap and down steeply to the main stream. A word of warning here. After very heavy rain or melting snow, the stream can be a torrent. Remember that this sort of water has immense strength, and do not attempt to cross. Cut the walk, and return down the valley. Normally, however, it is very easy to cross, using the rocks in the bed. A faint path climbs steeply round the spur of the hill and then up and across the hillside, with lovely views down the valley. From the head of the side clough, there is no path, but the going is quite reasonable. Follow the lip of the moor in two curves, west then northerly, to Wet Stones. From here turn west for about 100 yards to pick up a shallow channel in the peat cover, which leads up to High Stones on Howden Edge. This is a superb airy viewpoint, looking over the Upper Derwent Valley, and across to Bleaklow and Kinder. Most walkers will wish to linger to absorb it all.

When you tear yourself away, turn about, and walk almost due south along the very edge to Row Top. There is a ruined wall, which is a good guide for the descent. Keep on the north side of the stream, and you should pick up a useful path leading down Howden Clough to the forest. This is a very attractive little valley, in contrast to the high edges.

From the foot of Howden Clough, there are no problems at all – just a pleasant, easy 2½ miles, with lovely views over the water, along the reservoir track to the Derwent dam. This stretch of water was used in making the 'Dambusters' film, with the Lancasters flying low over the water. Just before the dam is reached, take the stile on the right and the path down to the road.

Grindleford Station, Padley Gorge, Higger Tor, Stanage Edge, Burbage Rocks, Longshaw

Although the outward and return routes are not far apart, the scenery is different and varied throughout. There are no difficulties, and the whole walk is over clear paths and tracks, but it should be noted that the higher parts (i.e. Higger Tor, Stanage Edge) can be in mist in poor weather conditions. There are approximately 900 feet of ascent from the starting point to Stanage. It is suggested that the walk be avoided on Summer Sundays and Bank Holidays, as – since Sheffield is almost on the doorstep – certain parts of the route become rather crowded on those days.

Parking is available opposite the old Grindleford station booking office, and the walk starts over the railway, turning left and then right up into the woods of Padley Gorge. This is a pretty section, with attractive views of the stream through the trees – plenty here for bird-watchers in Spring. The path leaves the woods higher up, but still runs alongside the water, before crossing it to the main road. Almost opposite the route continues, crossing Burbage Brook again, and climbing up the hillside clearly to Carl Wark, a prehistoric hill-fort. Some of the original wall stones still stand, and the defensive position is obvious, but one wonders how they fared for water under a long siege. The vegetation is now heather moorland, with some forestry in the valley eastwards. The path to the rocks of Higger Tor is clear, running somewhat north of north-west. It is worth arranging a rest here as the views are excellent, especially westwards over the Derwent Valley.

The path continues in the same direction, crossing one minor road, before joining a second one. A few yards along this road, after turning left, the route to the end of Stanage Edge starts away to the right. Stanage is a very fine gritstone edge running north for over three miles, almost to Moscar, with magnificent crag and rock – used a great deal for climbing. There are some fine examples of completed mill-stones lying discarded under the edge in the northern half. The views are absolutely superb in clear weather, with vast stretches of high moorland from Bleaklow Ridge in the north, south to Kinder Scout and beyond. Those with plenty of energy will probably like to walk part way along the edge, and return to savour the splendour. It is interesting to note that the Roman road from Brough (Navio) to Templeborough crosses the edge in the dip about half way along.

Leave the rocks on the path running almost due east, down the hillside to the road near the bridge. A few yards beyond the bridge, take the track on the right gently downhill under Burbage Rocks. This is a pleasant easy section, through heather and bracken. The main road is reached very near the point where it was crossed on the outward journey. Take the path almost opposite, crossing the second main road (the A6011), and proceeding on the delightful path along the front of Longshaw Lodge. This is an old shooting lodge, and in the past access was very restricted, but now many paths are open to the public.

Continue walking with no real change in direction to the road. Turn right for a short distance, but before reaching the Grouse Inn, turn right on a field path. (If you are thirsty, and the hour is right, you can of course proceed to the pub for refreshments). The path runs almost due west and shortly – quite dramatically – reaches the edge of an old quarry, with very good views over the valley towards Sir William Hill. Turn right at the quarry and follow the path down through the woods, and eventually round the back of some houses to the road. A right turn here takes you to the main road, where after a short walk downhill, you can turn right to the starting point. The old booking office, waiting room etc. is now a café, and with a bit of luck, tea will be available.

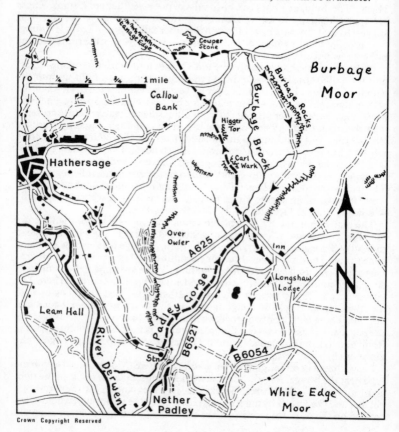

12

Westend Forest Gate, Alport Castles, Grains in the Water, Bleaklow, Grinah Stones, Barrow Stones, Westend Valley

Most of this walk is over wild, rough country, often without any real path, and it is essential that the walker should carry a compass and that his equipment, food etc, should be in accordance with the rules of mountain safety. Futhermore all people attempting the walk must be sure they have the ability to complete it – there is no bus they can catch half way round – no road either. Having said that, the walk is an adventure into a very real – if fairly small – wilderness, with superb views, and a fine sense of solitude.

The walk starts at the end of the west-pointing arm of the Howden Reservoir, just before the bridge, and limited parking is available on the left of the road before the forest gate. Take the track through the gate, and just over the first stream, turn left steeply uphill on the sign-posted public footpath. The gate at the end of the forest is the access point to open country, and the route is clear ahead up to Alport Castle. This is said to be the largest landslip in Britain, and certainly provides some spectacular crag. The views too are extensive – westwards to the Kinder plateau, and south over many well-known hills.

From here is a real departure for the wilderness. Behind are the green fields of the Ashop and Alport Valleys – ahead is desolation. Walk north-west alongside the wall, and continue on the lip of the moor as far as two small side streams (often no water flowing). Just over the second stream bed, turn north for a short distance, away from the Alport Valley. You should pick up a path turning north-west on the ridge to the Trig point. Continue north-west on the path, but just before the ground becomes much rougher, with many groughs, turn almost due west – no path – and head for the upper part of Miry Clough. Just beyond this clough, it is best to lose a little height, down to the clear path running half way up the eastern hillside of the Alport Valley. The gorge-like valley hereabouts, and indeed all the way to Grains in the Water is very impressive with lovely waterfalls and waterslides. Grains in the Water is a pleasant watersmeet of Hern Clough and the Alport and is a serene place in the high hills. The Pennine Way from the summit of the Snake Pass is half a mile away en route for Crowden and human figures can sometimes be seen on the skyline.

A shortening of the walk can be made here for tired people, cutting out some rough ground, by following the Alport almost to Alport Head – see map. For those with plenty of energy, take the faint path on the east side of Hern Clough. About 300 yards beyond the point where the Pennine Way comes in, and well short of Hern Stones, turn out of the clough and walk north-east over rough ground. Fork Stones, high on the hillside should soon become visible ahead, with Grain Stones to the east. Walk along the hillside under Fork Stones and

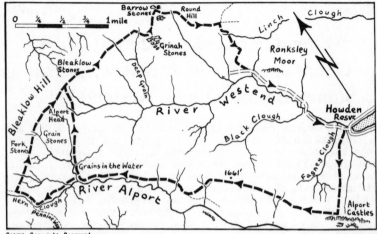

into the gullies of Near Fork Grain. Navigation is a bit tricky here, and unless you know the area, it is best to walk by compass north-east to Alport Head. Turn east out of the stream bed and walk high along the hillside, crossing the head-waters of the Westend River, before turning north-east again to Bleaklow Stones. At 2,060 feet, this is the second highest point in the Peak District (parts of the Kinder plateau are a little higher) and the views are extremely good.

Grinah Stones – the next objective – can clearly be seen (except in mist) to the east. The easiest route is to leave Bleaklow Stones, walking somewhat south of east, and losing height until a reasonable path is picked-up running on the contours along to the steep-sided gully, which is the head-waters of Deep Grain. A clear path curves round to Grinah Stones – a nose of impressive rock jutting into the lower moorland. Walk over the top to the south facing side. The view from here is, in the writer's opinion, one of the best in the Peak District. The whole line of the Kinder plateau is visible to the south-west, with Lose Hill poking up behind Crookstone at the eastern end. Win Hill, and half the hills of Derbyshire lie ahead, with the superb line of the Eastern Edges to the east.

A rather disjointed path runs north-east to Barrow Stones – another good viewpoint. Barrow Stones are really a whole stratum of gritstone lying on the hilltop, carved by erosion into fantastic shapes – they are worth a look. Note too the massive Crown Stone looking across to Round Hill, which is the next section of the walk. There is a good view of the Derwent Valley from Round Hill. A ninety degree turn – to south-west – is needed to follow the faint path down to Ronksley Moor. At the foot of the slope, turn south-east on the faint-and wet-path. Continue on this for half a mile, until a deep narrow channel appears on the left. There is a similar channel, but not as steep sided on the right. Walk along this, and you will soon join a clear shooters' track. Navigation problems are now over. Follow the zig-zag track downwards into the Westend Valley, where it leads back to the starting point.

14

Edale, Kinder Scout, Crookstone Knoll, Edale

On a first visit to the Peak District many people look for a spot they have heard referred to as The Peak. What they eventually find is a high plateau – that of Kinder Scout itself, once forbidden territory.

Kinder is best approached by train to Edale where, on leaving the station, we turn left up the road. If arriving by car, turn right out of the car park and pass under the railway. On our right is the National Park Information Centre where advice, maps and guide books are available. Or route starts from the timber bridge over Grindsbrook, reached by continuing beyond the Old Nag's Head Hotel to the point where a path drops steeply to the river and the bridge itself.

This, according to which way one is travelling, is either the start or the finish of the 250 mile-long Pennine Way route from Edale to the Scottish Border. A well-worn footpath across the meadows takes us over a stile, through a copse, over another stile and out on to the hillside, where we follow, at varying heights, along the side of the brook until, in a mile or so, we reach a fork in the stream. Taking the left fork will get us to the edge of the plateau. Then we bear slightly left and follow the edge track to Crowden Tower. Here, we have extensive views across the Valley of Edale, with the Lose Hill – Rushup Edge ridge in the foreground on our left.

Continuing by Edale Head and Noe Stool, we follow the plateau's edge track round to Swinesback (from afar it looks like one!). Here the route turns North and passes the trig stone of Kinder Low on the right. Half a mile to the north-

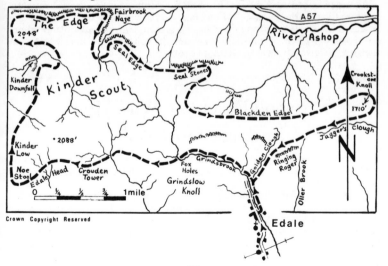

east is the highest point in the whole of Peakland, "The Peak" on the old maps, at 2,088 feet.

With the west wind beating on our left cheek and panoramic views of Hayfield (a good starting place, too) below us, we are now heading for Kinder Downfall – a mere trickle of water over smooth rocks in summer, but a glorious cascade with rainbow sprays or a frozen mass of gleaming icicles in winter.

Resisting being tempted into bogs by inviting sheeptracks, we turn north-west at the Downfall and follow the track round the Edge to Fairbrook Naze, the steep escarpment overlooking both Ashop Clough and the Snake Pass, keeping the latter in view all the time now as we swing along by Seal Edge, Blackden Edge and Crookstone Knoll – the plateau's eastern limits. The plateau is almost a ridge in itself hereabouts and if the day is clear there are some notable landmarks to be seen: Bleaklow plateau unfolds across the Snake Road. To the right is Derwent Edge, with Ladybower Reservoir nestling in the valley. South-eastwards lie Win Hill and Bamford Edge.

It is time we were heading homewards and our path lies on the southern edge of the plateau – above the head of Lady Booth and Oller Brook – to where Golden Clough drops steeply away from Ringing Roger's shapely outcrop into a gliding descent back to Grindsbrook. We then rejoin our original path at the stile into the woods and back to Edale.

For those who traverse the whole round of this plateau, no less than 15 hard miles will lie behind them at the finish. The less ambitious need not be overawed by distances, however, for this circular walk can start and end at many of the points indicated. In addition to the Edale starting point, for instance, Hayfield and the Snake Road form equally good starting and finishing points, though it must be remembered that public transport on the latter road is almost non-existent.

Access points to the Kinder plateau are now numerous and are indicated by signs on the moorlands as well as on National Park maps to be found in many places in the district. During the shooting season, many of the upland moors are closed to walkers for one day a week and the voluntary wardens who patrol the area will give advice as to alternative routes.

Route 7   **8 miles**

Errwood Reservoir, Wild Moor, Burbage, Goyt Valley

This walk commands views of areas which remain immune from indus-trialisation. The moorland section contrast well with the milder scenery of the Goyt Valley.

Commence walking from the car park on the west side of Errwood Reservoir at a road junction where a Roman road known as The Street climbs out of the valley. Descend to cross the reservoir embankment and follow the road round Bunsal Cob. Notice the plaque opposite the public conveniences which informs us that the road was built on a former railway incline – the famous Cromford and High Peak. Continuing uphill, there is a signposted path on the right heading towards a plantation and clearly marked by way-mark posts. After passing the plantation, the path descends through fields to reach the old Goyt's Lane, which now disappears into the depths of Errwood Reservoir.

Cross over the lane and take the track signposted "Goyt's Clough". Where the track turns right over a bridge, keep straight ahead upstream on a clear path. This is Wildmoorstone Brook. The path descends to cross a stream in another ½ mile then climbs steadily uphill, bearing slightly left near the top of the rise. Here we cross the abandoned railway near an old tunnel which is now sealed.

Follow the wall ahead to the top of the hill then just after a guide post the path bears slightly to the right and crosses rough grassland. Make for the ladder stile at the right edge of the wood. Descend steeply, with good views over Buxton ahead of you, to join a lane at a signpost.

Turn right down the lane for ¼ mile to reach a cottage on the left hand side just after passing through a gateway. Here turn sharp right and climb up the lane past a farm to join the Cromford and High Peak trackbed again which we turn left along for ½ mile of level walking.

The rough, stony lane we now encounter was the Buxton – Macclesfield turnpike now replaced by the road just across the valley. Heading towards

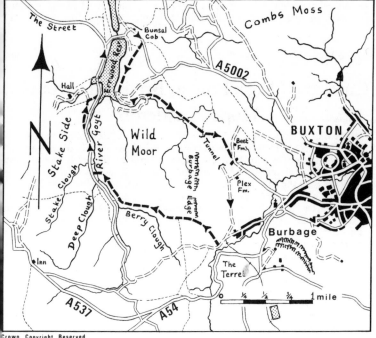

17

Macclesfield, we soon turn off to pass over a wooden stile on the right with a signpost. The path runs alongside a wall beside trees, then turns right with the wall and runs parallel for a short distance before aiming to the left of some trees on the skyline. Cross the step-over stile here over a wall, heading west over desolate moorland.

The "Cat and Fiddle Inn" can now be seen on the skyline at an altitude of 1690 feet, the second highest public house in England. Shining Tor is just to the right of the Inn. The path soon becomes stony and turns northwards temporarily to cross a small stream then west again. Continue to descend gradually beside a stream into the Goyt Valley.

Do not cross the footbridge but continue downstream on a narrow path through bracken on a level with the metalled road. Look out for a path turning off on the left and doubling back to cross the Goyt by an old stone packhorse bridge. Previously within the site of Errwood Reservoir, this bridge stood on a former Saltway.

Continue down the valley along the road through an attractive area among trees. After about ¹/₂ mile a track leads off to the left through a gate, soon affording tantalising glimpses of the reservoir through the trees. On reaching an open view of the reservoir, turn down through a large field to rejoin the road at a car park. This is the starting point of the Errwood Hall Nature Trail where one can see the ruins of a what was a fine Victorian mansion. See notice board in car park for details. Turn left along road to reach our starting point in ¹/₂ mile.

Route 8   **13 miles**

Castleton, Peak Forest, Bradwell, Brough, Hope, Castleton

A walk which includes the castle of Sir Walter Scott's "Peveril of the Peak"; a village that was once a sort of Gretna Green and a Roman military station.

From Castleton car park, turn left into the main street then right along Castle Street. Pass the village green to reach the signposted path into Cave Dale. As you progress up the dale, be sure to look back to see the remains of the Norman keep of Peveril Castle on the heights above the dale. Ruined and incomplete though it is, there is sufficient structure remaining to make the steep walk up to the Castle Keep well worthwhile at the end of the walk if time permits.

Pass through iron gates, gradually gaining height to where the path merges with a broad, grassy track. After a short climb, make for a gate in the top corner of the field passing some old railway wagons. Go through gates to turn right along a walled lane. To the right is Rowter Farm with Mam Tor as a backcloth. Keep forward with the wall on your left for about ¹/₂ mile. Mount the stile beside the iron gate then a second stile immediately to the left.

The path we now follow is signposted to Peak Forest and runs generally south-westwards with good views ahead. Cross a leadmine rake at some trees and keep straight ahead to cross a broken wall. Conies Dale is to your left and

18

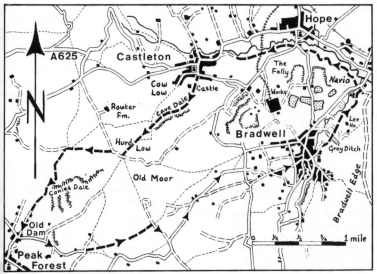

Peak Forest ahead as the path bears away slightly right. Just before reaching a dew pond, turn off left from the distinct path to pass over a broken wall and pick up a faint path leading down to a wood and stone stile, heading directly for Peak Forest. Cross two fields by the wall on your right and continue downhill through two more fields to a gate at a farm. The rutted lane takes us to the hamlet of Old Dam.

If it is desired to visit Peak Forest continue straight forward along the road for quarter of a mile. The church is dedicated to Charles the Martyr and it was here, in the original chapel, that runaway couples were married.

Back at Old Dam, pass the old hand-pump and climb eastwards along Old Dam Lane for just over ½ mile. When the road turns away to the left, go over two stiles and turn half left along a wooden fence to a stile over a wall then diagonally across two fields to a small ladder stile in the top left hand corner. Keep in the same direction to another ladder stile, heading for trees on the skyline. In the next field we pass to the right of a stone barn near old mine shafts and on to a ladder stile at the trees. Continue uphill by old mine tips with the wall close on the left. Turn sharp right after crossing a ladder stile, along a lane at opencast workings.

There are good views here including Lose Hill, Win Hill, Derwent Edge and Stanage Edge. Turn left on reaching the metalled road. This is the Roman road, Batham Gate which we follow downhill, passing more opencast workings. Eventually we come to a cross-roads where a short-cut back to Castleton is possible on turning left along a road. Our route goes straight across and on down a narrow lane with Bradwell Edge ahead of us. Turn left on reaching another metalled road to descend fairly steeply into Bradwell.

Cross over a rushing stream by the public conveniences to reach the main street. Go straight down the lane opposite (Soft Water Lane) for about 30 yards to a stile on the right. Follow the clear path from stile to stile passing over an old earthwork known as "Grey Ditch" then cross two driveways and pass to the right of Lee House. Cross a small stream to a stile, then go straight ahead over two stiles, the second one by an iron gate. Follow the track to cross another stream at a gate then proceed to a second gate. Keep along the side of the hedge to a signpost where the track turns left to skirt round the edge of the field. A stile beside a gate gives access to a lane which we turn right along passing some cottages. Take the turn left then go left again on the B6049 road.

A signpost on the right points the way up the valley to Hope and Castleton. The path now cuts through the field occupied by the Roman fort "Navio". The dressed stones mark the site of the Praetorium on our left. Leave the fort by crossing a small footbridge and then, keeping a wire fence on your left, go through several fields until you reach a stile amongst a group of trees. Over the stile is a grassy track which is still part of remains of the Roman road 'Doctor's Gate'. Follow this to the road. On reaching the road, go right down a lane then left at the junction of the road leading to Pin Dale.

In 30 yards take the path on the right at a stile, following the river upstream through four fields then across a railway line. Continue along the obvious path, passing Peakshole Water and eventually joining the main road into Castleton. The car park is at the far end through the main street on the right.

Apart from visiting Peveril Castle, it is worthwhile seeing one or more of the five caverns in the neighbourhood which are open to the public. These are: Treak Cliff, Speedwell, Blue John, Treak Cliff Hill and Peak Cavern. The latter is quite close to the village and runs under the ruins of Peveril Castle. Castleton itself has several interesting old buildings and merits exploration if time permits.

Route 9   6½ **miles**

Foolow, Great Hucklow, Abney, Bretton Clough, Breton, Foolow

The delightful compact little village of Foolow comprises the church, chapel, hall, manor house and inn, all encircling a green complete with cross and village pond. At the base of the cross a bull ring set in a stone reminds us of an old barbarous pastime. There are others at Eyam nearby, and at Snitterton near Matlock. This walk climbs past the gliding club on Abney Moor to Abney, crosses the depths of Bretton Clough, and returns over Eyam Edge.

Take the Great Hucklow road from Foolow green, and in a short distance cross a stile on the right. After crossing three fields the path joins a green lane which leads into Grindlow. On the road, go straight ahead, ignore a left turn

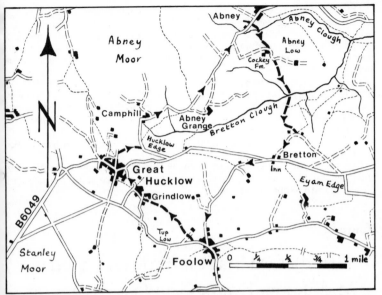

and at the T junction at the main road, turn left into Great Hucklow. Turn right opposite the Methodist Church, and at the end of the road turn right up a path beside the school. Turn left off the path at a stone pillor and climb to the road.

This road leads left to Abney, passing the gliding club on the left and revealing panoramic views over the hills with Bretton Clough cutting deeply on the right. Abney Grange is seen down on the right, and then the next farm is Cockey Farm which is on our route. The road drops steeply to cross a wooden glen, and where it leaves the trees and the houses of Abney come in sight, a stile is seen on the right. The signpost reads 'Public Footpath to Nether Bretton'.

Over the stile the path drops to cross the glen, and at the top of the steep bank a step stile leads into a field. Keep to the fence on the left, bear away round the field to cross a dip and climb the hill, when Cockey Farm comes in sight. Aim across the field towards the farm and a stile is found, and from here the path goes to the farm road seen to the left of the farmhouse.

This was the birthplace of William Newton (mentioned in Route 11). Son of a carpenter, self educated, he became a poet and eventually the successful owner of Cressbrook Mill. He became known as the 'Minstrel of the Peak' and of course still is.

From the farm, leave the road by forking slightly right to a corner of the wall and a stile. Over the stile, follow the wall on our left to the edge of Bretton Clough. Pause here and define the route as follows. From the bottom of the clough below us, it climbs to the right of a line of trees on the far side, to the corner of the field behind them.

21

The path drops steeply through the bracken to the clough bottom, bearing slightly right as it zig-zags up the far side to a wooden stile. Over the stile, the path leads to a stile in the corner of the field previously mentioned. Cross the stile, follow the wall on the right, and in the next field aim towards the house seen ahead. A stile to the left of the house leads through the garden and into a lane.

Turn right to pass a new hostel of the YHA and on to the main road at Bretton Here is The Barrel Inn, perched high on Eyam Edge at more than 1300 feet above sea level. Since 1637 it has stood here, seen on the skyline from far away in many directions. The road along the edge climbs to Sir William Hill on the left, and to the right Great Hucklow. The view to the south is wide panorama of fields and white walls, with the houses of Foolow seen among the trees about a mile away.

There is no way across the fields to the village, so turn right down the road and soon fork left, the road ahead clearly seen and providing an easy and pleasant return to our starting point.

Route 10   **8½ miles**

Grindleford Station, Froggatt, Stoney Middleton, Eyam, Grindleford Station

This is a walk from Grindleford Station which contrasts the pleasant Derwent riverside scenery with the breathtaking views over the valley from the higher ground. We visit the pretty village of Froggatt, Stoney Middleton with its tepid springs, unusual church nave and Corn Laws repeal cross, on to Eyam, a village of great antiquity and its claim to fame for its self-sacrifice over 300 years ago during the Great Plague, and back to Grindleford via Padley Hall.

Leaving Grindleford Station by the main approach, join the road leading down past the Maynard Arms Hotel to the bottom of the hill passing St. Helen's Church (erected 1909) on the left, and the restored toll cottage on the opposite side near the bridge. Turn into the field on the left by the stile and follow path over a stream and along the wall side of a smaller field into Froggatt Wood. This is National Trust property. The path continues across three fields and enters an occupation lane which leads into Froggatt. Across the river to the right Stoke Hall may be seen among the trees. Continue through Froggatt, cross the bridge over the Derwent on the right, and immediately strike left down worn stone steps into the riverside field, branching diagonally right once through the next stile to cross another stile in the far corner. Follow along the side of the wall up to the road (B6001), cross and continue up the lane to Knouchley Farm. Pass to right of farmhouse and turn diagonally left across field towards two adjacent gates. Go over a stile at second gate and follow path alongside wall bearing left away from wall downhill to reach the boundary wall to Stoney Middleton Hall. At the end of the wall cross stile into lane leading into Stoney Middleton and note stone trough on right beyond two houses. This is fed by a warm spring which also supplied the ruined 'Roman' baths nearby. After a few yards turn left to reach the entrance of St. Martin's Church (15th Century tower and curious octagonal nave built in 1759). Turn right after church gate and continue through village to main road (A623) and the cross erected in 1846 to celebrate the repeal of the Corn Laws. Turn right along main road and first right by small octagonal building. Go up hill a short distance and then sharp left continuing uphill passing telephone box on left and small chapel on right to a stile and footpath marked by finger-post to Eyam. Cross style and up grassy path. Stop and look back at views over Stoney Middleton and Calver. At top of slope cross stile into walled lane, through squeezer and follow track into Eyam village. Note graves of two plague victims on left. On reaching village cross road to see the Bull Ring. Continue up Church Street to explore rest of village; 12th Century church with Celtic Cross (800AD), unique sundial on church wall, plague cottages, stocks and old market hall etc. Retrace footsteps along Church Street, passing Bull Ring, to end of village. At end of houses take lane to left of main road (F. P. Riley Graves) and beyond Riley Graves fork right at finger post and follow path down through trees and continue down to road (B6521). Turn left along road for about ¾ mile and

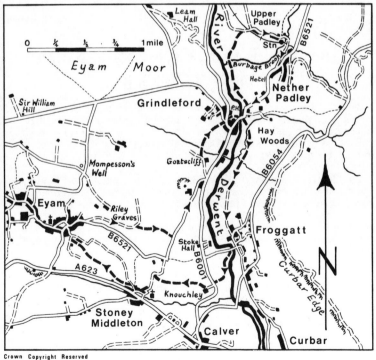

23

a few yards from junction take lane to left past Goatscliff Farm. At sharp right bend in lane go over wooden stile on left and diagonally left down field to Goatscliff Brook. Cross brook by stepping stones and go up field keeping wall on right for 100 yards. Go through Squeezer and keep hedge on left. Then through stile and keep wall on right. At corner of field take squeezer to right and follow path to next stile. Follow path round derelict barn, through wooden gate and out through iron gates to War Memorial at foot of Sir William Hill Road. Cross main road on to footpath beside Sir William Hotel. At end of path turn left on to road (B6521). Cross bridge and turn left on to riverside path opposite church. Cross bridge over Burbage Brook and continue alongside river to stile at end of next field. Over stile and sharp right up field keeping wall on right. Halfway up second field turn diagonally right towards left side of copse of trees. At fingerpost bear right through gate and follow grass road to railway bridge. Over bridge, turn right through gate and over cattle grid to Ancient Monument Padley Hall, scene of the story of the Eyre family and the Padley Martyrs in 1588, and opposite, Brunts Barn, restored and used as Ranger Volunteers and briefing centre. Continue on passing Padley Mill, over brook and railway bridges noting Totley Tunnel (1893) on left, and back to starting point.

Route 11   **7 miles**

Tideswell, Litton, Cressbrook, Millers Dale, Tideswell

Tideswell Church is popularly known as 'The Cathedral of the Peak', and before beginning the walk here, do have a look around it. From this limestone village among the hills, our walk goes through the next village of Litton, drops into the Wye valley by way of the not so well known Ravensdale, and continues through the lovely river gorge past two mills before climbing back on to the hills.

The George, a coaching inn of 1730, stands next to the church in Tideswell, and directly opposite its door, across the road, a narrow road is the starting point. This soon becomes a jitty (twichell or jinnell) as it climbs to the Litton road. Continue into the village with its modern church, pass the cross on the green and just pass the next turn on the right notice the oldest house in the village which faces down the road and has the date 1639. About 100 yards on, another house faces down the road, and here a stile is found beside it on the right.

Cross the stile, follow the path to the opposite corner of the field, cross a rough road and continue down the hillside into Tansley Dale. This runs into Ravensdale, and the path climbs the opposite hillside to join a path coming down from Wardlow, which drops steeply right down the side of Ravensdale. The dale becomes wooded, with high crags as it deepens. In the bottom, cross the footbridge over the stream (dry in summer) and turn left beside the wall to Ravensdale (locally 'Bury-me-Wick) Cottages, sheltering beneath towering

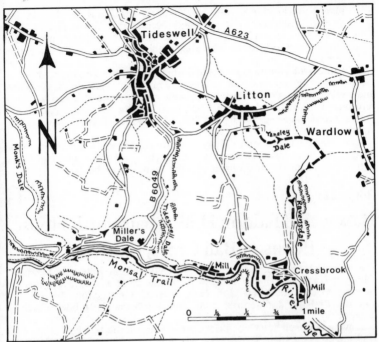

crags. From here an access road climbs to join another better road which drops left down to Cressbrook Mill.

Turn through the mill gateway and pass the mill, not one of William Blakes 'dark satanic mills', but looking more like a house for the gentry. Facing it is Apprentice Row where the children who were employed at the mill lived. The mill owner, William Newton, 'Minstrel of the Peak', whose birthplace is passed on route 9, treated his young employees well. Continue through the mill yard to the river, or more correctly, the mill dam. This lovely gorge is known locally as 'Water-cum-Jolly', but the water is no longer jolly, for the dam has created stretches of still waters which reflect the high limestone cliffs.

The path passes through the yard of Litton Mill, and it was here that child slavery was at its worst, as described by one of the unfortunates, Robert Blincoe in his memoirs. The book is obtainable at your library. The path between the mills is about 1 mile, and is private, with a concession to walkers, and one leaves it through the mill gates into Millers Dale. From here the dale has river and road for over two miles to the village of Millers Dale. This is our route, but at weekends, especially in the summer, it can be very busy with tourist traffic. But there is an alternative, and at such times one may prefer to use the quiet Monsal Trail, the route of the old railway which runs just above the river.

To take the trail, after leaving the gate of the mill, go forward to the last building on the left where a signpost points over the mill dam to the trail. Here a plan of the route shown Millers Dale to the right, and there, at a similar plan, a path drops down to cross the Wye. Here, only a portion of mill wall, together with the mill race, remain.

Cross the road, climb a few steps to the higher road and turn right. About 50 yards ahead a narrow road forks left beside a row of cottages. This is our route, and it climbs on to the hills laced with white walls for a quiet leisurely 3 miles return to Tideswell, strikingly different from the wooded Ravensdale on the outward route. Bear right at the first fork, pass Meadow Farm seen on the hill, and soon the village comes into view.

Ignore the next lane going off right, to turn right at the T junction into the village. Continue forward, ignoring a turn right, after which any road to the right takes one into the main street with the church up to the left.

Route 12   **9 miles**

Bakewell, Haddon Hall, Chatsworth House, Edensor, Ball Cross, Bakewell

Starting at Bakewell, this route goes from the Wye over the hills to the Derwent, calling at Haddon Hall and Chatsworth House (if so wished). It passes the Bowling Green above Haddon Hall, Russian Cottage on the edge of Chatsworth Park, and returns from Chatsworth via the model village of Edensor.

Leaving Bakewell Square by Bridge Street you pass the 17th century Market Hall and cross the River Wye to turn right along the old coach road. You leave it by turning right at the railway bridge where the Monsal Trail begins – or ends – on the route of the old railway. Continue along the lane and then cross a stile on the right, dropping down a short field to a footpath beside the river. Turning left you join Haddon Park Lane.

For those wishing to visit Haddon Hall cross the lane to a stile and follow a well-worn path in the valley bottom, crossing the river to emerge on the A6 Bakewell-Rowsley road, turning left for about 400 yards to the hall. (about 1½ miles return trip to Haddon Park Lane).

To give Haddon Hall a miss (little can be seen from the road and you need a long visit to appreciate this fine medieval hall) turn up Haddon Park Lane and after it curves over a tunnel of the old railway look for a notice on the right indicating 'Public bridle road'. Entering the gate, follow the railings to Bowling Green Farm; obviously a building of some importance.

The farmhouse, originally a pavilion to the bowling green in front, was built by the 18th century owner of Haddon Hall for the pleasure of his friends. Little can be seen because of the high wall, but the ornate entrance to the green with steps and ball-topped pillars can be seen over the iron railings as one approaches.

Turn left beside the wall, and soon the path becomes a rough farm road, bearing right as it tops the hill. Ignore a right fork, and here a fine view opens up

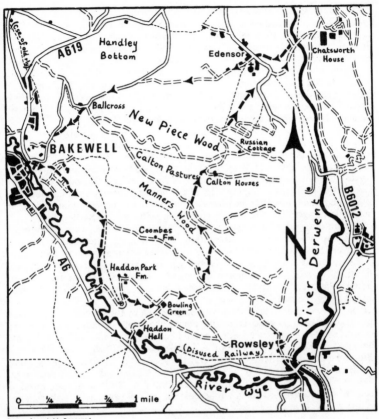

on the left with Bakewell seen in the distance down the valley. Pause at the T junction a little farther on. Here in the solitude of these hills and woods it comes as a surprise to know that the rough road coming from Rowsley on the right and down to Bakewell seen on the left was once the main turnpike up the Wye valley before the A6 was built in the valley bottom past Haddon Hall. At that time the route we have just walked past the Bowling Green was the drive down for Haddon Hall.

Cross the old road to enter an open gate into Manners Wood on the left. The track ascends steeply to join another track which is followed for about 100 yards before striking up the right again, eventually running beside a stone wall. The way continues between banks of bracken (in season) to an open gateway in the wall, and here on the left a gap in the trees reveals an even more magnificent view down the valley.

Pass through the gateway and turn left through a plantation of young conifers. The path leads in about 350 yards to a gate in a corner, but turn sharp right 12 yards short of the gate along a wall side to a stile into Calton Pastures. Here an extensive panorama is revealed. It is always interesting, and useful, when confronted with a view like this, to identify the route ahead, if possible.

The skyline across the valley is fringed with the edge of New Piece Wood, two thirds of it on the left being conifers and the rest deciduous. The noticeable gap between them is our route. The black and white house seen on the right is Russian Cottage, a replica of a Russian-style house of timber built by the 6th Duke of Devonshire to signify his friendship with the Tsar.

To cross the valley, proceed downhill obliquely left till a signpost is reached. This indicates a bridle path into the valley bottom which crosses the gully and here you leave it to turn right beside the wood to Calton Homes, continuing left beside the wall. With Russian Cottage in sight you bear left to the gap in New Plantation Wood already referred to. The road through the wood leads into Chatsworth Park, with a superb view of the woods, gardens and great house. It should be understood that the public are admitted to this particular area of the Park by kind permission of the Trustees of the Chatsworth Settlement.

Here a notice board with a map shows that the area of the park down to the River Derwent is now open to the public. Thus footpaths detailed in previous editions of this book are no longer necessary and one may head straight down to the house. Returning across the bridge, leave the road and take the path climbing the hillside to the right over the hill to Edensor. This model village of so many architectural styles was built by the 6th Duke about 1839 to replace the old village he had demolished.

Pass through the village, but do not be deceived by the precise, picture book appearance, for this road is an old packhorse route, a fact which is more acceptable as one leaves the houses and it becomes a rough lane. Where it joins the good road from Pilsley, an old milestone of 1709 reads Bakewell, Chesterfield and Sheffield. Over the hill, the road descends to turn steeply right past Ball Cross Farm, and on the left at the turn a gate leads into a rough road.

Here are two signs, and our route is the right one, leading into the wood to cross the golf course and join the road near the old railway station. Bakewell lies a short distance down the road.

Route 13   **8¹/₂ miles**

Fox House Inn, Froggatt Edge, Froggatt, Padley Gorge, Fox House Inn

This walk starts at Fox House Inn, originally a shepherds cottage built by Farmer George Fox in about 1773 and thought later to have inspired the "Whitecross" of Jane Eyre.

Enter Longshaw Estate by gate directly opposite Fox House Inn and follow path to join main drive at the Lodge Cottage. Note old stone signpost and spelling just inside gate on right.

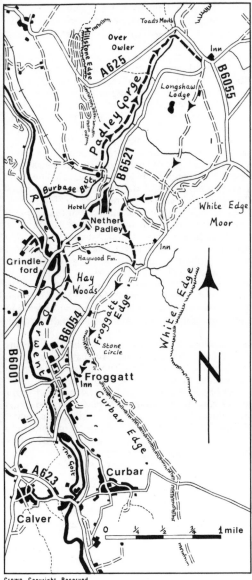

Crown Copyright Reserved

Continue down drive and branch right down steps (signposted) on to path in front of lodge (N.T. shop and tea room) to left and sweeping moorland views to right. Pass through two wooden gates and follow grass covered drive noting lake on right. Having passed between two isolated gate stoops the path continues to right of fence bounding woods to a gate intersecting the drive. Go through gate and shortly at double bend in drive descend through wall on step-stile to right into rough moorland field. Follow path down slope in direction of left of copse. Cross stream at bottom of dip and continue forward up-hill keeping wall of copse on right. At break in wall and gate on right, turn left through gap in wall opposite the gate and cross field towards rocky out-crop to a ladder stile in right-hand corner of field at foot of rocks. Cross ladder stile and continue on line of path up slope keeping rocks on left and on to Tumbling Hill. Follow grassy path round rocks looking down right on to

Grindleford and River Derwent. The path deteriorates into rocky uneven track on hillside through deciduous woods. As path improves note natural pinnacle of rock on left, and on leaving the rock faces take right fork by silver birches and on over stile into car park.

Follow path through trees to right of car park passing signpost and continue in direction of Froggatt Edge. At end of car park cross stile and at far side of dip ascend steps on to road (B6054). Turn right and then diagonally left across road and through gate to open country along Froggatt Edge. Follow well defined path along edge with its splendid views of the River Derwent meandering below between tree lined banks, and Win Hill through valley to right with Kinder Scout in the far distance. Soon after crossing small stream proceed through gate and look for bronze age stone circle just off path to left. Continue to reach an isolated field with dry stone wall to left of path. At end of wall follow stony path down diagonally right to ledge and rock faces on right which are extremely popular with rock climbers. From here there are fine views of the river and village of Froggatt below and the stone quarry of Stoney Middleton at far side of valley. About 50 yards before reaching the Pinnacle (a pillar of rock standing away from rock face with a number of unfinished mill stones around the foot) drop down diagonally left on rough path through trees, mainly birches at this point, and continue downhill through woods to a wooden stile. Go over stile and continue downhill to reach a road (B6054) a short distance from the Chequers Inn. Cross road and stile beside gate ahead and continue downhill and through a squeezer stile on to road. Turn right into Froggatt village passing bridge over River Derwent on left and views up to Froggatt Edge on right. Where road turns right uphill by Wesleyan Chapel, keep straight on along lane parallel with river a couple of fields down on left. Go through stile and at end of wall on right across field diagonally right through stile and follow wall on left.

Cross next field starting on slab path and over stile at far side into Froggatt Wood (National Trust). Follow path through woods crossing stream by old stone bridge and at end of woods follow path beside wall on left to small wooden gate. Go through gate, over small streams and cross field to reach the road (B6521) at Grindleford Bridge opposite the restored toll house. Turn right along road passing St. Helen's Church, and a few yards past Maynard Arms Hotel turn left along station approach road (pillar box set in wall on right). Cross bridge over railway with the old Totley Tunnel (built 1893) on right, over Burbage Brook and pass Padley Mill, an old wire drawing mill, on right. Just past Padley Mill turn into rough lane on right and proceed up slope and through gate into Padley Gorge (National Trust). Follow path uphill through woods looking down on fast flowing Burbage Brook and series of waterfalls on right below. At end of woods continue along beside brook noting Burbage Edge, Karl Wark (ancient hill fort) and Higger Tor dominating skyline ahead. Pass wooden bridge over brook and sluice gate, and cross brook at next wooden bridge. Ascend stone slab path and where path crosses small stream turn right over small waterfall. Looking back through trees across brook, Toad's Mouth Rock can be seen beside road in distance. Follow grassy path through trees towards Longshaw Lodge, seen across fields ahead, through gate, across road to right back to Lodge Cottage and turn left up path to Fox House Inn.

Bakewell, Monsal Trail, Monsal Head, Monsal Dale, Ashford, Bakewell

The Monsal Trail, that portion of the route of the old railway from just below Bakewell to the Wye Valley and on to Millers Dale and Buxton, has opened up a new path and fresh views to the walker. This walk is easily followed from Bakewell along the trail to Monsal Head, down Monsal Dale and through Shacklow Wood to Ashford-in-the-Water and Bakewell.

From the 17th century Market Hall with its mullioned windows and gables, (information centre for the Peak District National Park) continue down Bridge Street and cross the 14th century bridge over the Wye. Go straight ahead up the hill to the station. Take the trail past the station, and in about 1¹/₄ mile Hassop Station is reached, rather surprisingly standing in open countryside. The reason is that it was built at the behest of the Duke of Devonshire to serve Chatsworth House, which lies about 4 miles away over the hills.

The next station is Great Longstone, with Stonebridge Hall close by. A little further on where the trail emerges from a cutting, a footpath from Ashford to Little Longstone crosses, and where the trail leaves the railway route we turn right across the fields to Little Longstone. On the road turn left to Monsal Head.

One of the show viewpoints of the Peak District, Monsal Head, or Headstone

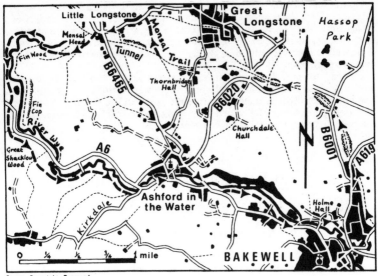

Head, is very accessible, and there are always visitors here enjoying the magnificent view down into the valley of the Wye. Down on the left the river passes under the railway viaduct to sweep round the base of Fin Cop. One might here reflect that when the high viaduct was built it caused a fierce outburst of anger from John Ruskin, a long tirade ending with the scathing comment "and now every fool in Buxton can be in Bakewell in half an hour, and every fool in Bakewell at Buxton; which you think a lucrative process of exchange – you Fools everywhere." It is ironic that were it ever suggested that the viaduct be demolished, there would be some objections.

Where the road turns sharp right to descend into the dale, a stile with signpost is seen on the corner. Through the stile turn left to drop down through the trees on the slopes of Fin Cop to the river. Cross the footbridge and turn downstream to climb a foot stile over a stream and go up a short field to the main road.

Cross the road to a picnic area, turn left in it for a few yards and then right up the bank to a stile. Follow the path marked "No 3" which turns left into Great Shacklow Wood, passing an old bobbin mill with latticed windows and twin water-wheels. Proceed through a stile to cross the fields and reach the Sheldon road which drops down left to Ashford-in-the-Water.

Turn right on the bypass for a short distance, and turn left over Sheepwash Bridge. The name comes from the enclosure at the side where sheep were penned and forced into the river. Today it is protected, being an ancient packhorse bridge. Call in the church opposite to see the old funeral garlands, once carried at the funerals of village maidens, for you will see them in only two other Derbyshire churches.

Continue down the street and turn right at the Devonshire Arms to a T junction. Cross the road to the old unused road which crosses the river over a bridge inscribed "M. Hyde 1664". Here Mr. Hyde lost his life when his horse leapt the parapet into the river. Pass through a gate on the left into a field which is crossed to the river, until near the weir the path crosses a swampy field and climbs a slight rise.

Proceed through five small fields and cust across Lakeside Estate and another field to join the main road which is followed left to Bakewell. On a right bend into the town, turn left over the river (a packhorse bridge of 1664) and turn right past Holme Hall. Turn through a stile into the meadows and follow the river to the bridge near Bakewell Market Hall.

Route 15   10½ **miles**

Cat and Fiddle, Cumberland Clough, Three Shires' Head, Axe Edge Moors, Berry Clough, Goyt Valley

This is an extremely attractive circle, which includes some very varied valley and moorland scenery. The route is entirely on paths and tracks with no really

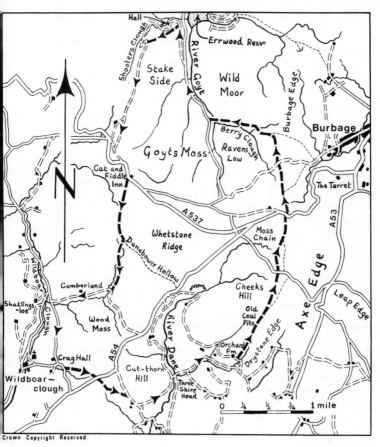

rough going, but it should be noted that the higher parts can be in mist, so a compass should be carried. The three main valleys visited are Wildboarclough, the Dane, and the Goyt, with easy climbs in between – a climb too in the last section back to the starting point. There are approximately 1600 feet of ascent in the whole walk. For walkers exhausted after the first six miles, there is an easy way of cutting short the walk.

Parking is available opposite the Cat and Fiddle Inn, and the walk starts from the car door on a clear path running south, with good views. After half a mile turn right off the Danebower Hollow path (signposted) down Cumberland Clough. The descent is quite steep for short sections, and the path crosses and recrosses the stream before joining a clear track at the gate, which leads down to the road. Note the pretty gorge on the left, and the views of Shutlingsloe across the valley ahead. Turn left on the minor road along to Crag Hall. Turn left again at the next road junction, but a little way up the hill, take the path on the left climbing up the hillside. The path goes straight across the A54 main road, crossing some fairly wet ground, before joining the track (by a house) leading down to Three Shires' Head. This is a very attractive area of field, stream and moorland, with lovely views south to the Roaches – linger over it. The narrow bridge over the Dane was an old pack-horse route westwards to the Staffordshire and Cheshire towns, and one of the items carried was the low-grade coal from the small pits higher in the hills. It is also said that the area was much used by the cock-fighting fraternity, who hopped from one county to another when one set of policemen approached.

Take the track running east on the Derbyshire side of the stream, and follow it for nearly a mile until a road comes in from the right – Orchard Farm is on the hillside. Turn left here, over the stream, and through the gate on the right. Be careful to turn half-left near the old coal shafts, and climb to Cheeks Hill. A stile leads on to a path to the road, where quick right and left turns are needed to join a clear track running north, eventually crossing the A54 and on to the old Macclesfield-Buxton road – this was the old coach road before the modern route with easier gradients was constructed. Note that a turn left here on the track, provides an easy walk back to the car – a useful cut-off for tired walkers.

Those still full of energy should continue north on the path, with lovely views, for half a mile before swinging west down Berry Clough into the Goyt Valley. Turn right on the road down the valley – pleasant walking through the trees. Watch for a gate on the left, and take the track almost parallel to the road. Further along this track, there is a pleasant view down to the Errwood Reservoir, enhanced I think by the coloured sails of the boats often sailing there. Just before the trees begin on the left (unless you wish to extend the walk by visiting the ruins of Errwood Hall – and the cemetery), turn left away from the reservoir, and climb the fairly steep hillside. The path eventually joins the wall above Shooters' Clough and follows it for some way. After a gate (with a path on the left heading back into the Goyt) a clear track leads to the main road with a short walk up to the car.

Route 16   **8 miles**

Longnor, Earl Sterndale, Hollinsclough, Longnor

This walk takes us into the upper reaches of the beautiful Dove valley around the twin Chrome (locally pronounced "Kroom") and Parkhouse Hill on the Derbyshire/Staffordshire border. We also visit a village with an unusual pub sign and make Longnor, once an important market town, the starting point for our walk.

In Longnor market place notice the Market Hall dating from 1873 before taking the lane to the right of "The Grapes" public house. At the crossroads a short diversion may be made to the church where a variety of quaint epitaphs can be seen in the churchyard. Our route is straight ahead on to a narrow lane then sharp right up a grassy track just after passing some cottages.

The lane has high grassy banks and ends at a stile with signpost. Aim roughly half-right across the field to a wooden stile and a fine view into the Dove Valley. High Wheeldon is the prominent hill in front across the valley. Now zig-zag down the hill to join a track down to a barn and turn left then immediately right through a stile by the side of the barn, where it is often rather muddy.

Continue forward through fields to cross the Dove at Beggar's Bridge thereby entering Derbyshire. Walk along the green lane until a stony farm road goes off on the left. Pass through a gate and follow this road for ¹/₂ mile, passing one farm to a cottage with an old water pump. A signpost on the right points the way through a stile to Earl Sterndale. Note: It is possible to cut out part of the walk if desired by keeping to the valley and passing through Glutton Bridge to the foot of Parkhouse Hill to rejoin the route there.

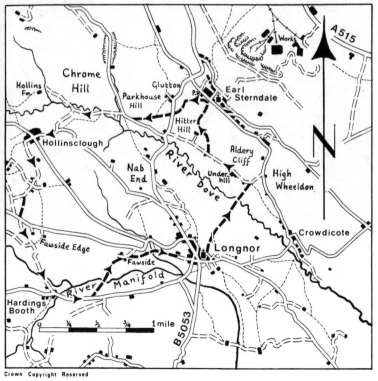

35

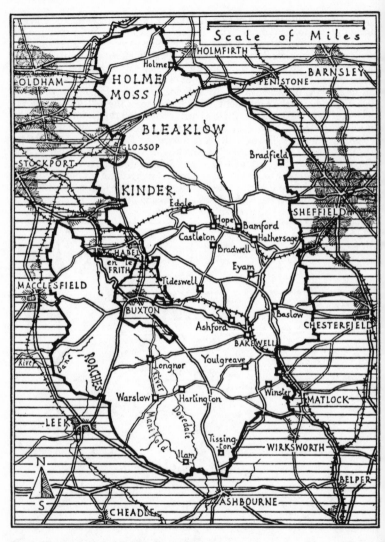

THE PEAK DISTRICT NATIONAL PARK

The Earl Sterndale path heads for the top left hand corner of the first field to a wooden stile, turns left climbing north-westwards up to a wall, and then continue alongside the wall to a stile. A pause to catch the breath here and enjoy the fine views. Continue to another stile, still following a wall then descend through fields to Earl Sterndale below. The 'Quiet Woman' public house has the unusual pub sign of a woman with no head – the only possible explanation!

Back at the side of the pub, there is a path which runs between sheds and walls passing a signpost to enter a large field. Alternatively, if there is difficulty, turn left from the 'Quiet Woman' down the road to a stile by a gate on your left after the first house. This is the same field mentioned above. Cross fields with Parkhouse Hill straight ahead and Chrome Hill visible to the right, the remains of coral reefs in the sea. Descend to the B5053 road near Glutton Grange.

Go straight across the road and through a stile then follow the path ahead through more stiles until a metalled road is joined on the south side of Parkhouse Hill. When the road bends right keep straight on to a track which passes between stone gate posts. Cross the river Dove by a substantial footbridge and so re-enter Staffordshire. Continue along the track avoiding the private road to Hollins Farm and join the lane into Hollingsclough.

At the centre of this little hamlet, go straight ahead up a farm road, taking a left fork just past the farm. The narrow, stony lane climbs gradually soon giving good views across the valley. Soon the lane becomes metalled and the route is straight on at the cross-roads and over a stile on the left just past a house. The path keeps close to the wall on your left through fields to a road. Almost opposite, a lane descends to Hardings Booth, a delightful walk of about half a mile.

Turn left at the next road junction for a quarter of a mile then take a path on the left at a gateway just as a small wood begins on the right of the road. Head roughly straight for the farm in the distance (Fawside), crossing the River Manifold by a footbridge. Pass in between the farm buildings along the farm road to where it swings left. Go forward through a field beside a wall on your right, through a gate and down to cross a stream. Straight ahead to the next stile then bear right slightly to a squeezer stile.

More stiles lead into a lane at Gauledge and on into Longnor Market Place in another quarter mile.

Route 17   **12½ miles**

Wye Dale, Deep Dale, Chelmorton, Flagg, Taddington, Millers Dale, Chee Dale

This circular walk starts at Wye Dale car park opposite Topley Pike, 3 miles from Buxton on the A6 towards Bakewell. It links the old mining villages of Chelmorton, Flagg and Taddington and descends into the Wye valley through Millers Dale, Chee Dale and back to Wye Dale.

From the car park beside the river Wye cross the road (A6) and through the

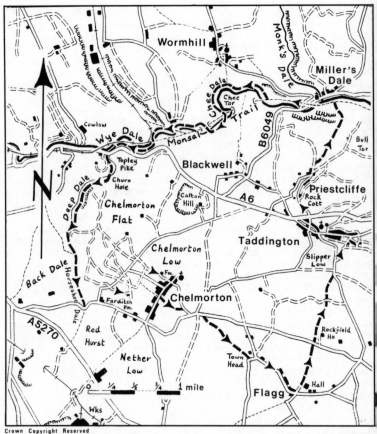

entrance to Topley Pike Quarry following signpost to Chelmorton. Keep to left
of quarry road and works, and in a short while to left of stream and wall. At the
end of the works where the path bears left into Churn Hole, go right over wall
and up steep slope to left of man-made earth barrier at end of Deep Dale. Pass
settling pool and follow path down into Deep Dale. Proceed the length of the
dale on path to left of wall and stream passing cave in rock face on left and
Ravens Tor on right until fork in dale is reached. This is the junction of Deep
Dale, Horsehoe Dale (to left) and Back Dale (right fork). Fork left along
Horsehoe Dale passing Bullhay Dale with its old mine entrance on left and out
on to road (A5270) between farm buildings. Turn left along road for short
distance and left again at first turning by Farditch Farm. At double bend in road
enter rough lane on right and at end of lane go ahead through gate and

38

diagonally left across field and through another gate into a rough lane at far corner. Continue along lane to right towards Chelmorton Low in near distance. Cross minor metalled road and at junction turn right passing Chelmorton Low with its tumuli and Shepley Farm, and into the village of Chelmorton. This is the highest village in Derbyshire at some 1200 feet above sea level.

Turn right into village leaving interesting church (part Norman) behind, passing school on right to reach footpath signs left and right of road. Turn left through two fields and over stile on to road. Turn right and at road junction bear left to cross transverse road. Turn right over stile at corner of second field. The path crosses the field diagonally left passing corner of field on right to a stile in the far corner under a solitary chestnut tree. Follow in same direction through shallow mining outcrop and then uphill and over a stile at a kink in the wall. Head for gate to right of small copse and then bear right to stile on to road at sharp bend with farm buildings to right. Cross road and follow line of path through fields until it converges with road into Flagg. Join road through village to reach junction, school and telephone on right. Turn left into tree lined lane and through farm with farm buildings on left and Hall on right. Follow footpath with wall to right, pass dew pond and across two more fields and on to road (A5270). Turn right and left over stile in a few yards into narrow field beside coal works entrance. About halfway along second narrow field cross stile over wall to right and follow path diagonally left across old mine workings to stile in next wall and continue across fields and stiles on this general heading for about half a mile until road is reached. Over stile on to road and turn left (signposted Taddington). After two fields on right bear right down rough lane and turn left into village of Taddington, an old mining village some 1,100 feet above sea level. The church on the right which has some unusual features, was rebuilt in the 14th century while the village was prospering from lead mining. The tower and spire were dismantled and rebuilt in 1866. Bear right past church and turn right into small lane at bus stop. Cross main road (A6) and follow minor road opposite into Priestcliffe. Shortly after another minor road converges from the left, bear left at junction by Lydgate Farm and over a stile on right, a short way down lane. Cross field diagonally left and continue on this route until border of Derbyshire Wildlife Trust reserve is reached at head of old quarry overlooking Millers Dale and Monks Dale in the distance.

Turn right and follow path down sharply beside the old quarry safety fence and out through trees on to the Monsal Trail (route of the old railway). Turn left along trail, cross bridge over river Wye and road, and turn left along old station platform. The station buildings have been converted into Peak Park Rangers centre and public toilets. Continue along trail and at next bridge turn right and then left down steps to river below. Turn right upstream along river bank keeping river to left. Pass footbridge and continue on same side to bend in river at Wormhill Springs. Cross springs and continue along river bank beneath spectacular rock faces rising either side of river. At next footbridge cross river and turn right under railway bridge to follow along opposite bank for short distance and then back again to North bank. Follow this path, which in two places becomes a series of stepping stones under steep escarpment and on under two railway bridges, to reach a wooden footbridge near some cottages. Cross bridge and follow unmetalled road back to car park.

Monyash, Lathkill Dale, Alport, Youlgreave, One Ash Grange, Monyash

Lathkill Dale, high among the best of Derbyshire's lovely limestone dales, is here traversed from above the source of the river, to its confluence with the River Bradford. The villages of Alport and Youlgreave are passed through before a return to Monyash is made over the hills, a fine 12 miles walk.

A look at the map shows this can be made into two circular walks of 4 miles and 8 miles, by using the footpath in Cales Dale where the outward and return routes of the full walk come within about ¼ miles of each other. The 8 mile walk starts at Alport (parking beside the road) while the 4 mile starts at Monyash, as does the full walk.

Less than ½ mile to the east of Monyash on the Bakewell road, a dip in the road indicates the beginnings of Lathkill Dale, a stile on the right giving access to it. Proceed down the field, ignoring a cart road on the right and continuing down the dale. Do not be put off by the waste from the Ricklow Quarry which has spilled down from above, for the effort is well rewarded later on. The going is still somewhat rough when the source of the River Lathkill is reached, issuing from a cave in wet weather, but rising from the river bed in dry weather a little further down the valley.

After another ½ mile Cales Dale joins the Lathkill from the right. For the short walk, turn up this dale to join the return route of the full walk at One Ash Grange.

Continuing down the left bank, notice the remains of an old corn mill still

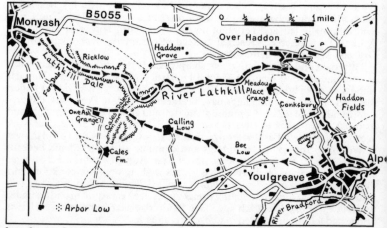

with its grind-stones, before entering woodlands in these middle reaches of the dale. The crystal clarity of the water will have been noticed, and in the 17th century, Charles Cotton (of The Compleat Angler and Izaak Walton fame) called it 'by many degrees, the purest and most transparent stream that I ever yet saw, either at home or abroad'.

Evidence of lead mine workings is noticed in the dale, and one should not venture into caves which may be open drift mines. The stone columns seen crossing the dale are the remains of an aqueduct which served an engine house beside the river, and there is much of interest for the industrial archaeologist. Farther downstream a footpath crosses over on a clapper bridge and here a narrow lane climbs steeply to Over Haddon between Lathkill Lodge and an old corn mill.

Soon the path emerges into a road at Conksbury Bridge, a narrow medieval structure which once carried the main road from Bakewell to Ashbourne via the Newhaven Inn. Turn right over the river and continue up this ancient way for about 200 yards to a stile on the left. From here the path drops to the river again near Raper Lodge, which featured in the film of D. H. Lawrence's 'The Virgin and the Gipsy'.

Where the path enters Alport village, cross the road to see the river tumbling down to meet the waters of the River Bradford. Pass through the gates on the right and follow the road which meanders beside the River Bradford beneath limestone cliffs. Soon a delightful packhorse bridge is reached with a track leading up to Youlgreave Church seen on the hill.

If you wish to see the church (it has a unique Norman font, among other things) deviate here, to join the main route later. Leave the churchyard by the same gate you entered, and continue along the village street to turn right at the circular conduit, (known locally as the Fountain) and in a few yards reach Old Hall Farm of 1630.

For those not wishing to see the church, continue beside the river, cross over a road and pass a clapper bridge to enter fields still beside the river. In a short distance turn up a well-defined path climbing obliquely out of the valley and into the village. Pass between the houses to the Old Hall of 1656 on the main road, cross over (slightly right) and go forward to Old Hall Farm where the alternative route meets.

The road climbs out of the village, and at a road junction (just beyond a car park) cross the road to enter the fields through a stile. The path is well trodden, and after passing Calling Low it drops steeply to Cales Dale with extensive views down into Lathkill Dale. On the other side of Cales Dale can be seen One Ash Grange, once owned by Roche Abbey in Yorkshire.

Cross Cales Dale to follow the cart track to One Ash Grange, noting as one enters the farmyard an arched entrance into an underground chamber with thrawls (food storage?) and a long line of interesting pig sties.

Bear right in the farmyard, and go forward uphill along a rough road to a gate on the right. Through the gate, turn left along the wall side and follow stiles to cross the head of Fern Dale and find a stile on the right. Over the stile, a gate is seen on the left where a green lane is entered. This soon becomes a cart track leading down into Monyash.

Monyash, One Ash Grange, Arbor Low,
Parsley Hay, High Peak Trail, Monyash

Derbyshire is rich in prehistoric remains, a look at the map revealing many tumuli or lows on the hill tops, and several stone circles. Arbor Low is the most important stone circle, but don't let the popular name 'Stonehenge of the Midlands' conjure up a similar edition of the famous monument on Salisbury Plain, for Arbor Low's stones lie flat. Nevertheless, it is well worth visiting, but first read a little about this mysterious 4,000 years old spot.

Leave Monyash by the Newhaven road, and where it bends right at the last house on the left, continue straight on along a rough road. Ignore the right fork. The road soon becomes a pleasant green lane which ends at a gate and stile. Follow the wall on the right, cross over a stile and cross the head of Fern Dale. Through the next stile follow the wall over the hill to join a rough road which drops down to One Ash Grange.

Do not enter the farmyard which leads down into Cales Dale and Lathkill Dale, but turn right along an open road which climbs the hillside. From this vantage point one can visualise these rounded hills alive with sheep long ago, when One Ash Grange was owned and farmed by Roche Abbey in Yorkshire. The road crosses the head of Cales Dale and passes Cales Farm to emerge on the good road at Long Rake.

The workings across the road are extracting minerals from the tailings or residue of the old lead vein or rake which runs for about two miles beside the road. A rake is a vertical lead-bearing vein of minerals perhaps hundreds of feet deep and running close to the surface, and the abandoned Long Rake is now being exploited for the valuable minerals in its waste heaps.

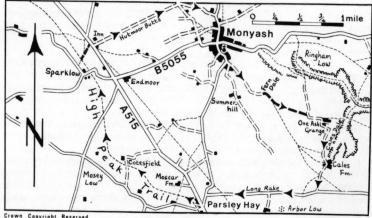

42

Turn right and in about ½ mile a farm road on the left leads up to Arbor Low. There is no need for a description here, but stand for a while on this exposed hilltop and try to imagine what kind of rituals may have taken place here about 4,000 years ago. The experts are divided in their opinions, although it is generally agreed that this was a religious site and the stones originally stood upright. Whatever the purpose of Arbor Low, one cannot but be impressed by the thought of people worshipping on this spot 2,000 years before Christ was born.

Back on the road, turn left to a T junction with the Monyash road (the village lies about 2 miles to the right) and there left to the Ashbourne-Buxton road. Turn left for a few yards and then right to the old Parsley Hay Station on the High Peak Trail. This, of course, was the Cromford and High Peak Railway which crossed central Derbyshire from Cromford to Whaley Bridge, a distance of 33 miles. Turn right along the trail for 3 miles of pleasant flat walking with embankments and cuttings opening up hitherto little known views of the surrounding hills.

Leave the trail just past the second road bridge by dropping down to the bottom of the embankment on the right side and proceeding to a kissing gate. Through the gate, aim uphill diagonally to an opening in the wall, continuing slightly right through stiles across the next two fields, and then aim towards a gate in front of the Bull-i-th-Thorn Inn beside the main road.

This roadhouse claims to date from 1472, and has an unusual sign, probably unique, carved in solid oak of a bull entangled in a thorn bush. Between the inn and a bungalow a rough road is our route, and runs straight for about 1 mile before bearing right to join the Flag road about ¼ mile from Monyash seen on the right.

Route 20   **6 miles**

Rowsley, Stanton Woodhouse, Stanton Lees, Stanton Moor, Rowsley

Although this walk is a short one, climbing from Rowsley to Stanton Moor, more time than usual should be allowed, for the moor is full of interest. This high gritstone plateau is a site of national archaeological importance with a prehistoric stone circle, several excavated burial chambers and other features of later date. Pleasant sandy paths through the heather makes the moor a place to linger and perhaps picnic. Naturally, it can be a windy place.

Turn off the main road opposite the Peacock in Rowsley, and drive over the River Wye to park the car beside the playing fields there. The walk begins along the road straight on from the bridge and soon climbs through the trees to Stanton Woodhouse. Where the hall drive begins, turn right, round an S bend, to pass between cottages and a farm where the road ends at a gate. Through the gate, follow the cart track round the hillside with fine views across Darley Dale. Just past a gate and stile the track forks and you take the left one to a fence slightly left of the tower seen on Stanton Moor. Where the fence ends go forward to join the road in the corner a short distance ahead.

Turn left and soon fork right into the village of Stanton Lees, perched on the steep southern slopes of the moor. Bear right through the village, the narrow twisting road climbing steeply and calling for care against the occasional car. The view down the valley of the Derwent is extensive, with Riber Castle as a backdrop to the Matlocks.

As the road nears the top a path (with a National Trust sign) leads up on to the moor. This path runs along the edge of the moor to the tower already mentioned, but continue on the road for a few hundred yards to the next path with a sign to the 'Stanton Moor Stone Circle'. Follow this path to the top of the moor, noting on the right (250 yards up) the laid open Bronze Age burial chamber. The tower over on the right was erected as a tribute to the Earl Grey who carried the Reform Bill through Parliament in 1832. Not far along the edge northwards from the tower, there are carvings expertly cut into the stones, one depicting a coronet over a Y with the date 1826, commemorating the famous Duke of York.

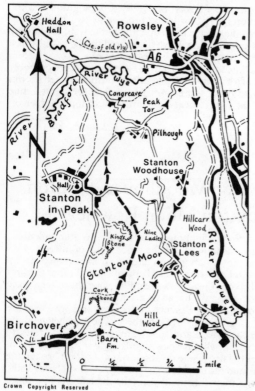

Back on the main path, the stone circle, the Nine Ladies, and the King Stone nearby, also from the Bronze Age, are seen on the left at the far edge of the moor. The path leaves the moor and becomes a cart track down to a road. Turn left and then leave the road along a track beside the wood on the right with the village of Stanton in Peak below. From the cricket ground here there are extensive views up the Wye valley towards Bakewell and an unusual view of Haddon Hall among the trees way down below. The path joins a road and Rowsley lies a very pleasant mile down to the right.

Matlock, Lumsdale, Cocking Tor, Riber, Matlock

This walk, east of Matlock, takes in the extensive mill ruins in Lumsdale, crosses the hills above Tansley and brings one suddenly to the breathtaking view of the Amber Valley from Cocking Tor. A close-up view of Riber Castle, built by John Smedley a century ago is a fitting end to the walk, for this splendid eye-catcher has been seen tantalisingly distant during most of this walk.

Leave Crown Square, Matlock, by the Alfreton Road. Where, after ½ mile the fields begin, take a footpath on the left beside the Scout Headquarters at the corner of Butts Drive. This leads to the road in Lumsdale. Turn left uphill between extensive mill ruins, and just past a sharp S bend a signpost on the right indicates a footpath to Tansley via Oaksedge Lane. Take this path, turn right on a rough road and then right again at a row of cottages to cross a mill dam, where it becomes a green track. It passes some old quarries with excellent views across the valley and the high ground beyond, soon dropping down towards Tansley. This joins a lane at some cottages and here you turn left with pleasant views across the valley of Tansley Brook as the lane twists and climbs. On the level it makes a sharp right turn to cross Tansley Moor in a straight line to a T junction. Here you turn left.

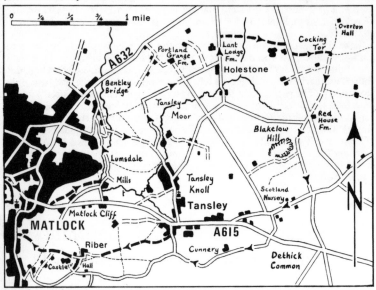

Crown Copyright Reserved

45

Four hundred yards up the road stiles right and left face each other. Take the path through the one on the right between a row of trees and the wall. Through the next stile follow the track beside the wall on the right to the valley bottom, and the footpath then aims diagonally across the fields towards the silo at the farm seen on the right of a spinney, and left of a wind pump. There are stiles in the walls, and at the last one near the wind pump go straight towards the silo and follow the wall to a stile and the road.

Turn right to Old Engine Farm where a sign opposite points down the side of a wall to a wood. Circle the wood and then aim for the far corner of the field to the right. Cross the stile here and follow the wallside, turning right with it to Cocking Tor, a typical Derbyshire gritstone escarpment with a superb view over the Amber Valley. This is the furthermost point of the walk and an ideal spot for coffee and those sandwiches – but a little exposed if it rains! Far up the valley to the left is Ashover, and in the middle distance below is Overton Hall, once the home of Sir Joseph Banks who sailed round the world with Captain Cook and whose name is commemorated in many far away places. Down the valley can be seen Ogston Reservoir, and immediately below us remains of old lead mines.

Follow the path which twists and turns through the heather along the rocky edge, and at the last massive rock descend a steep path to join a lane seen climbing a hill on the right. Follow the lane and cross over crossroads, ignoring the right fork immediately beyond and turning right at the next crossroads. On the left side of the road, about 300 yards down (opposite the far end of Scotland Nursery and below a new bungalow) notice an old guide-post dated 1719 now used as a gate-post. Its sides are marked to point respectively to Wirksworth, Derby, Chesterfield and Bakewell and it must have been brought here from elsewhere.

Take the next turn on the left and at the crossroads go straight on into Cunnery Lane, pass Cunnery Wood and continue to a T junction. Turn right and about 250 yards on take a lane to the left beside new bungalows. Where this short lane reaches the wall on the left, cross a very narrow stile and turn right alongside it. The path goes straight along the sides of fields, until after ½ mile a long field is reached lying at an angle to the line of the path. Go diagonally across the corner of this field and then straight ahead until a track leading into Riber Village is reached. Continue uphill between the cottages to Riber Castle.

From the Castle gateway a well-defined path leads down to Matlock, reaching the road beside the modern school. Turn right past the church and then left steeply beside the churchyard, then left into the public park and on to Crown Square.

Route 22   *Completed* 4/4/05.   **10½ miles**

Cromford, Slaley, Ible, Grangemill, Cromford, Black Rocks, Cromford

This walk climbs from the Via Gellia at Cromford on to the hills above, drops down to the top of the dale again before climbing past Aldwark to the High Peak Trail. Along the trail to Cromford Black Rocks, and down into Cromford makes an easy and interesting return.

From the Greyhound Hotel in Cromford take the narrow road on the right (Scarthin) past the mill-pond, and where it joins the Via Gellia road cross straight over to a path. Pass through a stile, then turn right through the trees with the brook down on the right. Where the path reaches the edge of the wood turn up the wall side to a stile. Over it you turn left beside the wood to where a well-worn path emerges over another stile. This you join by turning right down to the mill buildings seen in the Via Gellia where you cross the millpool onto the main road.

In this mill was first made 'Vyella', a corruption of Via Gellia, and it is interesting to note that this road was made by the Gell family of Hopton Wood. Philip Gell believed his family's ancestry dated from the Roman occupation, for a piece of Roman pottery was found bearing the name 'Gellius' hence the Latinised Via Gellia.

Cross the road to climb Chatterway (named from the time when this steep hill was made of loose stones?) and turn sharp left at the next turn (Black Tor Road) to rise steadily to Slaley, high above the deep wooded valley of the Via Gellia. Soon after leaving the houses turn right through a gateless gateway, from which a stile is seen across a narrow field. Stiles are followed through small fields completely disrupted by old lead mine workings. Most of the old shafts are now covered by concrete, but others still have their broken cairn of stones, and the many hollows may be the site of shafts covered only by turf on rotten timbers. The route is quite safe, but do not stray.

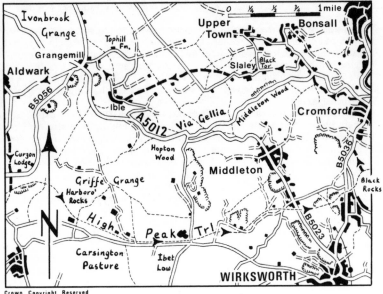

47

Where the path comes out on a road to the right of a barn, take the stile opposite and continue down the wall side to a farm. The walk passes behind the farm and continues beside the wall to drop into a dip and then climb over a low hill into another dip. Here the wall ends with a stile into the next field. Turn left up the hedge side, and where the hedge bends left continue straight on up the open field, and in a few yards a stile is seen ahead. This is the first of no less than 8 stiles in a distance of about 400 yards, so narrow are the fields! Through the last one an open gateway is seen down towards the village, and from this a stile can be found into the road beside a telegraph pole to our left.

Turn right to Ible, noting a row of 10 stone troughs in front of the old chapel – now a pleasant dwelling – and continue along the lane to turn left in Grangemill. Over the crossroads take the Ashbourne road and in a short distance fork right towards Aldwark. The road climbs steadily, fine views spoilt by a huge quarry works below, and at a road junction you turn sharp left. The road runs straight and just round a sharp bend a blocked stile is seen on the left. This was the route in previous editions of this book and here a sign indicates that the new route can be found further along the road. Here is a stile and you follow the wall on your right and then bear right across two fields before following the wall downhill. Longcliffe comes in sight below and you go straight down the last open field in the direction of a new car park which serves a large stone works. Crossing the road through stiles into the car park, you aim for the far corner to emerge in a rough track, crossing it slightly right to a stile. Diagonally across the field a set of steps climb the walled embankment of the old Cromford and High Peak Railway, and from here there are about 4½ miles of easy walking to Cromford Black Rocks. Today it is a trail, very popular at summer weekends.

It is odd to think that this route was first envisaged as a canal to link the Cromford and Peak Forest Canals, and one soon realises that the cuttings and embankments seen here would have made this an extremely difficult venture, together with the problems of water supply. Instead a railway was built, in 1830-31, and the waggons were drawn by horses to be replaced by locos in 1841. Even so, several steep inclines necessitated cable hauling and engines, and one is passed later.

Harboro Rocks are reached within about 1 mile, and they can be explored if wished, by crossing a stile just past the brickworks buildings. A shallow cave here was the home of man thousands of years ago, remains of animals now extinct in these islands have also been found. Two miles further on the Engine House and Information Centre come into view at Middleton Top, both open at specified times, and at the bottom of Middleton Incline (gradient 1 in 8 and ½ mile long). You are passing through the National Stone Centre, England's first stone museum, with access from the trail. Beyond lies Wirksworth.

Ahead is Cromford Black Rocks where the trail is left. Climb to the top for a fine panoramic view of the Derwent Valley, with Matlock Bath and Cromford far below and Riber Castle high on its hilltop. Leave the trail by passing through the gate on the left, and then immediately right down steps and through the trees to an open gateway on the left. A short track takes one to the main road, and Cromford lies ½ mile downhill to the right.

Ambergate, Shining Cliff Woods, Whatstandwell, Lea and Dethick, Bilberry Knoll, Cromford Canal, Ambergate

This walk may be taken in parts, a look at the map showing it forms the figure 8, the crossing at Whatstandwell could thus divide it into two separate walks. As with all walks, spring is a good time, but this walk is specially attractive then for the blue-bells in May. The scenery is charming, except for industry near Ambergate.

To get this over first, turn off the main Derby-Matlock road at Ambergate Church towards Shining Cliff Woods. These are National Trust property. Immediately after crossing Ha'penny Bridge (originally a toll bridge) over the Derwent, and the mill-stream, turn right. A the top of the rise, take the right fork down through the wire works yard, which makes no pretence but of being just that. The site has a continuous history as an iron forge from the days of the ancient Royal Forest of Duffield, of which these woods were part, and we are following one of its ancient roads.

Beyond the wire works the road ends at a gate with stile, becoming a path which climbs through unspoilt woodlands with the Derwent Valley below. Leaving the woods you enter Alderwasley Park and go forward to a clump of trees, continuing to join a farm road. Turn right past the War Memorial; the Georgian Hall seen below is now a Special School for Children. You join the road in Alderwasley over a stile. Turn right past the park gates and round the corner note the 16th century chapel of St. Margaret's on the left, renovated as a Village Hall.

The road drops pleasantly to Whatstandwell Bridge which you cross and walk up the road towards Crich, and in a few yards turn left (after crossing the canal) to Holloway. The road rises steadily through a wood, and where the houses of Robin Hood come into sight turn right up a path beside a lamp post. Continue forward through the old quarries now overgrown with fern, silver birch and mountain ash. Higher up the track cross a stream, and carry forward ignoring a stile on the left with the stream on the right.

Cross the stile at the end of the wood into a field, proceeding forward as though making for Crich Stand on the cliff in front. When about 150 yards inside the field bear left with the boulder strewn hedge (and stream) on the right, to cross a stile into the road. Turn left for about 30 yards, to pass through a stile on the opposite side of the road and aim to the left of Wakebridge Manor Farm. Follow the track to the left of the farm which is a medieval road leading straight to Dethick. Incidentally, don't be surprised to see a tramcar gliding along the hilltop on the right, for over the hill is the Crich Tramway Museum.

Where the enclosed track ends at an open gateway you turn through an opening

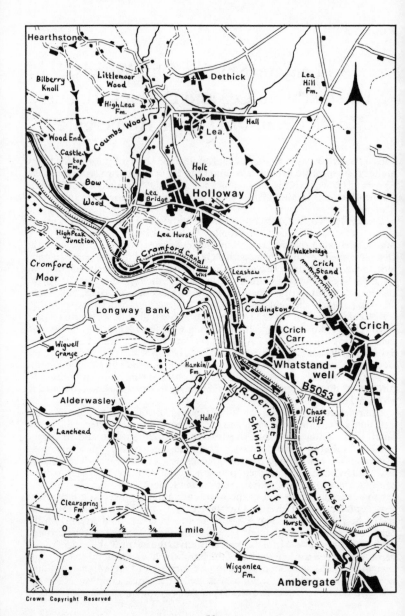

50

on the left. The path crosses the field obliquely to rejoin the same ancient track which goes on to a road. Cross the stile opposite when another stile across the field gives the line of the stiles through the fields to Lea. Within a couple of fields from Lea the path bears left towards a section of broken wall. It is on the edge of a sunken medieval road, Town Lane, which is followed right until, about 30 yards on, a stile high on the left side marks the continuation of the path diagonally across small fields towards a gate near cottages in the village.

Continue down a lane, and where it joins the main road, turn right past the chapel to a stile on the left, dropping into a little dell with a simple stone bridge over the stream. Out of the wood, follow the hedge on the left to join a path taking us to Dethick, with its church and Manor Farm. This was the home of Sir Anthony Babington of the Babington Plot against Elizabeth I (not a lot remains of the original hall) and much of the film 'Traveller in Time' was made here. Note that although a chapel has stood here for 700 years, there are no graves in the churchyard. The key to the church may be had at the farm behind, and a gate in the wall round the corner is the way to it. The country around here is quite unspoiled and lovely, with fine views down towards the Derwent Valley.

Turn down to the road and turn left as far as the T junction at the bottom of the hill. Turn left into the hollow to look at two very charmingly situated houses. Our way, however, is to the right past Littlemore Wood. There is no right of way through the wood so follow this pleasant lane towards Riber and then turn off just above a bungalow (Littlemore Cottage) on the left, along the farm track on the left to the little hamlet of Hearthstone.

At the T junction with Hearthstone Lane turn left to pass Bilberry Knoll and simply follow this grass-grown track down to Castletop Farm. Here are splendid views over Cromford towards the Via Gellia, and there is rarely anyone about to share them. Castletop Farm, seen on a knoll ahead, was the birthplace of Alison Uttley who wrote 'Traveller in Time' already mentioned, also 'The Country Child' and 'The Farm on the Hill', all set in this area.

On the good road just past Castletop Farm pass through the right of twin farm gates (on the left) along a track below the wall of an attractive cottage. The way leads through woodlands to Lea Bridge. Where the track emerges on the main road turn right downhill for 150 yards and turn left between stone houses. Within 30 yards cross a stream and turn left immediately alongside of it to round a cottage and continue up to the Leawood Canal. This branch of the Cromford Canal was built by the Nightingale family for their smelting works which stood behind the high wall we have just passed, and later a hat factory stood here where they made those little red 'pillbox' hats from the Crimean War. Continue along the raised towpath high above the River Derwent to the junction with the Cromford Canal. The ruined cottage on the left is the old lockkeeper's house, and the high building over the river to the right is the Leawood Pumping Station built to take water from the river to augment that in the canal. Cross the canal; the bridge is a copy of the original swingbridge which allowed the horses to reach the Cromford towpath, and turn left along the towpath, passing through a tunnel, and on to Whatstandwell and Ambergate, leaving the canal at a canal house and within sight of Ambergate along the main road.

51

Risley, Dale Abbey, Stanton by Dale, Risley

For this walk we leave the popular dales and moors of the Peak District and turn to one of the few areas of unspoilt countryside between the cities of Derby and Nottingham, However the walk is through pleasant countryside and is full of interest.

The way-marks that you will see on this walk referring to 'Circular Walk' do not apply to this walk, so do not necessarily follow them.

We start in the small village of Risley, taking the lane which leads north from between the church and the village school. Before leaving Risley it is worth having a look at the almost miniature church, the school buildings and the 'Latin House' the last two of which date from about 1710.

Follow the picturesque brook with the nature reserve on the right and immediately after crossing the first stile there is another one on the left which may be obscured by undergrowth in summer. Take this and follow the field boundary. When the hedge goes off to the right cross the field to the metalled lane. Turn right here and go up the lane as far as the small wood on the left. Immediately after the wood turn left after the gate and keeping the hedge on your left, follow the field boundary round over two stiles and then at the end of the next field turn left over the footbridge. Go up the hill from here, noting the fine view of the Trent Valley. Continue on over three stiles, past a coppice and continue westwards until you reach the farm track at Hopwell Hall farm.

Turn right and follow the farm track for nearly a mile until it reaches the road at Sandiacre Lodge. Go straight ahead along the road until another road joins it from the right. Go over the stile opposite this and follow the well worn path under the crest of the hill. Shortly you will see the hermit's cave carved out of the sandstone in the woods on your left.

The cave is reputed to have been made by a Derby baker who left his home in response to a religious vision in 1130 A.D. Having inspected this abode, pass through the farm and you will come to Dale church which is in fact the very unusual combination of a church and house under one roof. It is well worth asking for the key of the church at Abbey House (around the next corner) to see one of the few churches where the old box pews survive.

Follow the lane as it swings left and then right noting that many of the village buildings contain stones taken from the ruins of the nearby 13th century abbey, only one large window of which remains. Turn right at the T-junction, if you can resist the temptation of the Carpenter's Arms, and follow the road until it swings right. Carry on straight ahead along the metalled track, and when this swings to the left follow the footpath sign into the field. Bear slightly right across the field to reach the stile on the other side, then follow the hedge in the next field until you come to a stile on your right. Go over this stile and follow the track past the pond to the road. Take the road opposite and walk uphill until you come to a stile on the left which may be hidden in the hedge. Go over this stile, immediately over another stile and make for the wood diagonally across the fields. Walk along the side of the wood and then down the hill to the road via a gap in the hedge near the cottage.

It is about half a miles walk along the road to the unspoilt village of Stanton-by-Dale which is probably worth a visit. However just before the village centre you will see a kissing gate on your right. The route goes through this and up the obvious track to the highest point of the walk at the gnarled oak on No Mans Lane. From here, weather permitting, you will have fine views over the Trent valley and to the hills of Charnwood Forest and the South Notts Wolds.

From the oak tree take the path leading south, cross a field, a part of a golf-course, then two more fields heading for a farm. Skirt round the left hand side of the farm to reach the stile and then follow the farm track down the hill turning left into the field just before the first house. You are now back on familiar ground and after following the fields edge, all that is left is the short walk along the brook to Risley.

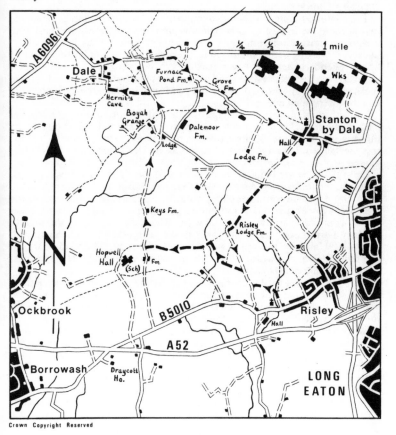

53

Ilam, Manifold Valley, Wetton, Alstonfield, Dovedale, Ilam

The beauties of Dovedale are shared equally by Staffordshire and Derbyshire, the latter county usually taking greater credit simply because the footpath runs along the Derbyshire bank of the Dove for most of its length between Beresford Dale and Thorpe Cloud.

The Manifold Valley – which also runs a parallel north to south course some two to three miles west of Dovedale – is entirely in Staffordshire, and both valleys comprise a limestone area of exceptional beauty. Here is some of the finest dale walking in this country, a fact very apparent at holiday times and on fine weekends, when the lower reaches can be crowded. For this reason weekdays are best – if possible – and winter times too, but it can be muddy then. A glance at the maps shows that Walks 25 and 26 link, thus covering both dales, and the intervening hills.

Drive through the 'model' village of Ilam with its gothic cross into the car park of the hall. There is much of interest in the grounds, so call in at the information shop here. There are Saxon remains at the little church close by, together with a fine large piece of sculpture by Derbyshire-born Sir Francis Chantrey.

Drop down to the bank of the Manifold where a few yards upstream the waters of the underground rivers Manifold and Hamps boil up from beneath the rocks. The path continues along 'Paradise', as it is here called, to cross the river over a footbridge. Ignore the footbridge seen across a field to the left. Stiles can be seen ahead to the top of a low hill where the way lies to the right of Rushley Farm. Turn left a few yards to the farm gateway then right up to Throwley Hall with the valley way down on the right. The road bears left through the farmyard where a footpath sign is seen on the right. Here you pass round a circular pond to a stile.

Here you aim for the lowest point on the skyline and from a stepstile there can be seen Beeston Tor down in the Manifold Valley. This is your route and you drop straight down the open field to join a farm road seen curving round the hill towards the tor where the River Hamps joins the Manifold. If the weather has been dry both rivers will have disappeared, having sunk into their beds higher up the dales, and their re-appearance has already been seen at Ilam. It is a curious fact that although they both join here in wet weather, their underground courses remain separate until they emerge at Ilam.

Cross the Hamps and go forward (do not bear left) along the route of the now defunct Manifold Valley Light Railway which has come down the Hamps Valley from Waterhouses. Easy walking through fine valley scenery takes one past Weags Bridge and in about one mile the impressive Thor's Cave is seen

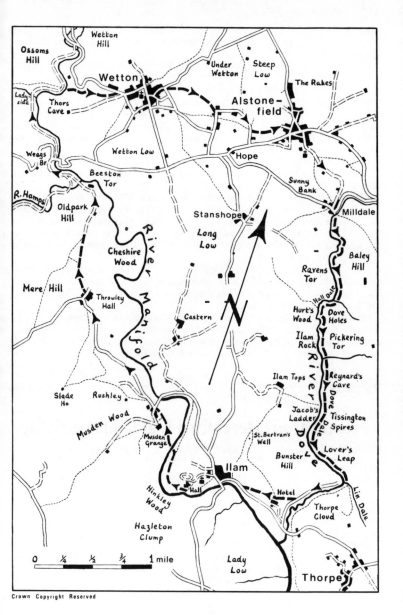

high on the right. Cross the river by the footbridge and climb steeply through the trees, staying in the dip through the fields to a stile on the outskirts of Wetton.

On the road go straight on past the church, bear right, and then turn left to pass a chapel. Where a road branches off right. Alstonfield, our aim, is seen across the valley among the trees. Cross a stile here and proceed down a dip through stiles into the valley bottom, bearing right to join a green road. Where this joins a good lane on a sharp corner, turn left for about ¹/₂ mile, ignoring two stiles on the left before crossing the third to climb into Alstonfield. At the last field, the stile is in the far left corner, leading into a short rough road which joins the main road.

Cross over the road and fork right to the church. This has the pew of Charles Cotton who sat here with his old friend Izaak Walton. In 'The Compleat Angler', Walton exclaims on first seeing this church; 'What's here, a church, do you have religion in these parts?' Past the church Mill Lane winds down to Milldale, but if so wished a footpath soon seen on the right takes one down through the fields. This little hamlet has a famous packhorse bridge, named Viator's Bridge, from a mention again in 'The Compleat Angler'. 'What's here, the sign of a bridge? Do you use to travel with wheel-barrows in this country? 'Tis but two fingers broad.'

Over the bridge, and on through Dovedale is sheer delight, with white pinnacles of rock, caves and the remarkable crag of Lion's Head Rock. Look for the plaque set on the rock, and see who we have to thank for making public so much of this beautiful area.

Pass the famous stepping stones and continue at the foot of Thorpe Cloud to cross the river over a footbridge. Here one may turn left to join the road to Ilam (right), or find a stile beside a car park entrance on the right to follow the path which crosses the fields behind the Izaak Walton Hotel into Ilam.

Route 26   **12¹/₂ miles**

Hartington, Beresford Dale, Alstonfield, Wetton, Manifold Valley, Hulme End, Hartington

This walk is complementary with Walk Number 25, and one should read the introduction to that walk. It will be seen that both walks could begin at Wetton or Alstonfield if so wished.

From the market place in Hartington go past the Charles Cotton Hotel to find a stile beside a public lavatory. Over the stile, bear right along a clearly indicated track soon to cross a rough cart-track running at right angles across the route. Continue through open fields for a short distance with a slight right incline, but head towards a tree-lined hillside in front, the bastion of Beresford

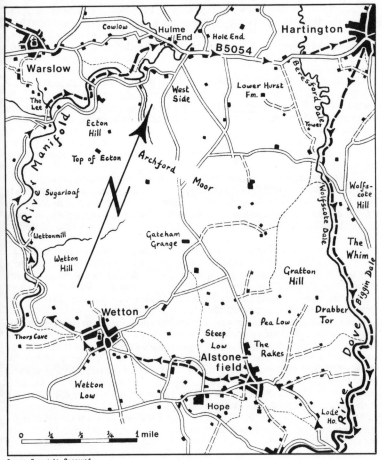

Dale, which itself is the first of half-a-dozen dales which comprise Dovedale area proper.

The River Dove is seen on the right, twisting its way across the fields towards the neck of a narrow passage through overhanging rocks in front, the beginning of Beresford Dale. Barely discernible through the trees on the far bank – and strictly private property – is the celebrated Fishing Temple (erected in 1674) which commemorates the association of Charles Cotton, of Beresford Hall, with Izaak Walton, whose exploits in the gentle art of fly fishing are immortalised in the 17th century classic, 'The Compleat Angler'.

Cross the river over a foot-bridge to pass Pike Pool, so named from the monolithic finger of rock rising clear from the water to a height of about 30 feet. Recross the river at the end of Beresford Lane and go forward across a meadow into Wolfscote Dale. From here it is about 2½ miles delightful riverside walking to Lode Mill, passing the end of Biggin Dale and Iron Tors at the end of a short dale lower down.

On the road at Lode Mill in Milldale, leave the river by turning right up the hill to Alstonfield. The church lies about ¼ mile along the first road on the left, but our route continues through the village to a junction. Cross the road to the Memorial Hall and take the rough road beside it to the fields. Where it ends, cross a stile seen on the left, going straight across the middle of the field (unless there's a football match in progress!) to find another stile. From here farm buildings at Wetton, our aim, can be seen across the valley slightly to the right.

The stiles are unmistakeable, and at a road, cross over to continue into the valley bottom. The path rises to cross another road and climbs up through fields to join the Wetton road from Hopedale. Turn right, keeping left at the next two junctions and then right and left in a very short distance. Turn right at the next junction and then left, leaving the village to drop down into the Manifold Valley.

High in its crag is Thor's Cave, where the remains of animals now extinct in these islands have been excavated, together with evidence of early man's habitation. Stories of ghosts and spirits once abounded in the area, and not unnaturally the cave has gathered superstitions around it. Perhaps the most popular is 'Fiddling Hobhurst', whose screeching on his fiddle in Thor's Cave years ago lead to its being called Hob Hurst's House.

Down in the valley, cross over the route of the old railway – or turn right along it – to Wetton Mill (refreshments) where there is a car park on the site of the station. Continue along the railway route, passing through a tunnel to see Ecton Hill across the river with remains of old copper mines once worked by the Earl of Devonshire and later the 5th Duke. Here the latter built a school, church and inn, but little remains of these. The hill is honeycombed with deep mines 200 feet below the river, and a huge water wheel 32 feet in diameter was installed underground to drain them.

The Manifold Valley Light Railway – the route along which we are walking – was built in 1904 in the hope that it would revive the copper and lead mines here, and also serve the farms and villages around, but it had little success and closed in 1934. Today the route is an easy flat walk through beautiful scenery through the whole of its length from Waterhouses (car park) on the Leek-Ashbourne road down the Hamps Valley to the Manifold and on to Hulme End.

On the road at Hulme End turn right for Hartington, crossing the river and passing the Manifold Valley Hotel to climb over the hill into the Dove Valley. The old corn mill beside the Dove is now a private house, and a stile is found beside the drive. Go through the stile cross the field to the middle of the wall, and from a stile here further stiles will be found in line with the buildings of Hartington seen ahead. And so into the Market Place there.

Milford, Chevin, Milford

Suitable for a pleasant summer evening, this is a short and interesting walk over the Chevin, with distant views of the Derwent Valley.

It starts from the Strutt Arms at Milford, the name reminding us that the mill, rows of cottages and the bridge, were built by Jedediah Strutt, about 1780 and onwards. Cross the main road and turn up Chevin Road opposite, turning left up Sunny Bank in about 50 yards to climb steeply to the Chevin. At the top the road becomes a rough track, and here stands a square stone tower, built by George Stephenson as a 'sighting tower' for his railway tunnel.

The track continues with a golf course on each side, climbing steadily along the ridge. This is a prehistoric 'ridgeway' a trade route in use long before Strutt or Stephenson came to transform the valley below, or the village of 'Muleford' was recorded in the Domesday Book. This 'ridgeway' is also thought to have been the line of a Roman road from Derby to Wirksworth. Soon the 'Butts' is seen on the right, a firing range used by local volunteers in the 19th century.

After proceeding level for about half a mile, leave the straight path by doubling back steeply up a rough track to the left. A short, steady climb leads to the rear of a covered reservoir, passing it to a sunken lane running down south of it to be the Belper-Farnah Green road. Turn left and ignore the road to Hazlewood on the right. In about half a mile the road dips steeply and bends right where a rough road goes off left behind Hazlewood Hall. Turn along this road to its end and take the narrow path behind the last house.

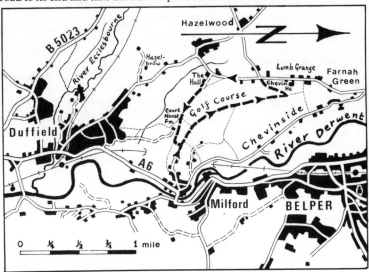

59

The older Ordnance Maps show this as an enclosed road running for about three quarters of a mile along the hillside to Courthouse Farm before turning up to the old track over the Chevin. Today it is completely overgrown as far as the farm, with a narrow path through the undergrowth. At the farm, the path comes out on to the golf course, with extensive views over Duffield. In medieval times this was a part of Duffield Frith, and at Courthouse Farm courts were held to settle infringements of Forest Law.

Where the path comes out at the farm, continue straight ahead across open ground for a short distance, turn left beside a wall and enter an enclosed track which leads up to the outward route track over the Chevin. In a short distance Sunny Bank is reached, dropping down into Milford.

Route 28 8½ **miles**

Allenton, Barrow-on-Trent, Swarkestone, Shelton Lock, Allenton

Although this walk begins in the Derby suburbs, it is more than compensated for by the Cornfields on Sinfin Moor and the walk beside the River Trent between Barrow-on-Trent and Swarkestone. For this reason the best time is in summer or harvest time, but certainly **not** in wet weather.

At Allenton, on the A514 south of Derby, go along Sinfin Avenue past the Memorial Village and where it curves left leave it to go straight on to the lane's end. Turn left along a path to cross the defunct railway line on the right, from which point can be seen Red Wood surrounded by fields of corn in season. Follow the path which passes towards the wood (under the power lines), cross a brook, continue beside the wood and hedge to cross another brook. With the hedge now on our left, cross two fields and another bridge seen to the right, into a rough lane. This improves as it climbs the hill to drop into the Trent Valley.

Cross the canal, railway and main road and continue to the church seen ahead, and round to the river. The road ends at a delightful group of cottages, a path going forward along the river bank and over a footbridge, to follow the river bank to enter Swarkestone between a white cottage and farm buildings. Turn right to the historic Swarkestone Bridge. Climb the bridge to see the long raised causeway built in the 13th century, the most southerly point reached by the soldiers of Bonnie Prince Charlie, who established a bridgehead here before their retreat from Derby in 1745.

Our route continues along the river bank to the church seen downstream, where there are fine monuments to the Harpurs who lived in the Hall nearby. This can be seen across the fields behind the church, together with the Balcony Field, and the old gateway to the Hall is seen at the main road ahead. Cross the road to reach Swarkestone Bubble on the Trent and Mersey Canal, here joined by the now derelict Derby Canal. Here we have a choice (see the map). We may cross the bridge and continue to a second bridge seen ahead, to follow the towpath of the Derby Canal towards Shelton Lock, linking up with the alternative route later, or a slightly longer route now described. Turn left along the towpath of the Trent and Mersey Canal past the lock-keeper's cottage, to the next bridge, here turning right up a lane to pass Swarkestone Lows, a farm taking its name from the ancient burial mounds seen in the fields on the right. The results of excavations by students and members of the Derbyshire Archaeological Society may be seen in Derby Museum.

The road becomes a track dropping to Sinfin Moor and joining a road where you turn right. Where it crosses a dyke you can take a footpath to Red Wood seen on the left and join the outward route. Joining the alternative walk at the Derby Canal you turn left along its route, now filled in, and cutting a green swathe through Shelton Lock. Where it crosses Boulton Lane you turn left back to the A514 road.

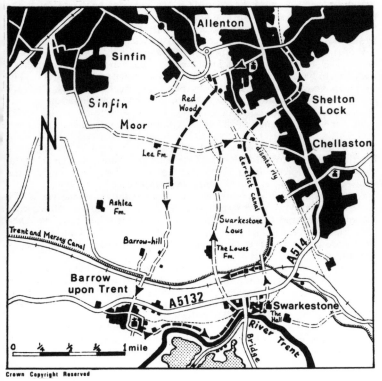

61

Repton, Bretby, Repton

The walk could start from point 'B' marked on the map, in which case a call to look around Repton could be made separately. This shortened version is 8¹/₂ miles long, but Repton should not be missed.

The shaft of an ancient cross on circular steps, the Parish Church and renowned public school are all within sight in the main street of Repton.

Retracing our steps past the cross we continue through the village until, just past the Shakespeare Inn, we find a Public Footpath sign beside the last house on the left. Follow the path, which crosses a stream and ends in an open area. Here stood an old mill and cottages mentioned in a previous edition of this booklet.

A stile is found on a low wall seen ahead, and once over it the path follows further stiles up the valley. Two new stiles of concrete – one on each side of the stream and private – mark the route of the pipeline from the River Dove to the reservoir at Staunton Harold. The last stile leads into a road which falls steeply from the left to a three-shaded bridge, a popular picnic spot with room to park beside the road. This is point 'B' on the map previously mentioned.

From this point, take the lane opposite the stile, which climbs between rocky banks to the hilltop. At the first farm here – Loscoe Farm – the road makes a right turn to Park Farm, but we continue forward down a pebbly cart track, its steep banks covered with blackberry bushes, young trees and hazels. The track crosses the valley bottom, passes Repton Shrubs, and climbs the hillside straight ahead.

On the hilltop we join a narrow road, with extensive views across the Trent Valley.

Continue forward on the road with the wood on the right, to turn right at a junction about half a mile on. Passing Greysich Farm there is another delightful view ahead as the road drops steeply into the valley where we turn right at the main road to cross a small bridge about 100 yards away.

A short distance past the bridge we turn up a rough track on the left. Where it ends at a bungalow, a narrow path goes straight ahead into a wood. We leave the wood over a stile, and in the field follow the fence which encloses ploughed land, the fence curving right to a stile which gives access back into the wood. From here a pleasant cart track meanders through the trees before descending to a lane on the edge of the wood.

In previous editions of this book is described how a narrow path re-enters the wood to climb steeply through the trees to emerge on the hilltop. Today a cart track follows the same route along a wide swathe cut through the trees. On the hilltop the track is enclosed by fences, going forward to the crest of the hill with wide views across the Trent Valley to the north.

This is Bretby Park, with open parkland dipping into the valley spread out before us. The path continues straight down the hillside towards the right of a wood and then round the last shoulder of the hill, when the impressive pile of Bretby Hall is seen across the lake.

Crossing the dam which forms part of a string of small lakes, we follow the track straight uphill to a plantation, bearing left round it to a gateway and the rear of the hall. We turn right down the drive, where in season there are usually conkers and sweet chestnuts.

A few hundred yards past the clock-towered building seen on the right, a stile is found with a path heading downhill towards the spire of Bretby Church. Over another stile we cross the road to pass the green with a covered pump (war memorial) and continue up to the church.

To the right of the churchyard gate a stile gives access to a field and here you turn left a few yards to another stile. The path being undefined we aim obliquely right to a clump of trees where a stile is found in the hedge. Over it we turn left, aiming for the bottom edge about 50 feet from the field corner, crossing a stile to the road.

A signpost indicates Repton as being 2¾ miles to the right, but this need involve us with only 1¼ miles on the road, and panoramic views across the Trent Valley makes this road walking very pleasant. Where the road drops into a valley a left turn at a T-junction brings us in a few yards to near the bridge at point 'B' mentioned in the outward route. If we have started from Repton, we can either continue along the road, or return along the outward route in the valley fields.

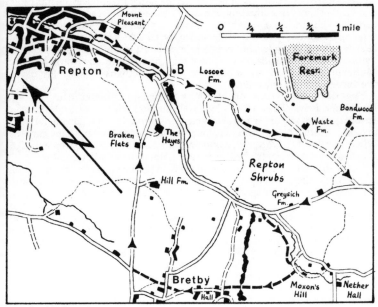

Crown Copyright Reserved

Markeaton, Vicarwood, Meynell Langley, Mackworth, Markeaton

From Markeaton Park in the northern suburbs of Derby can be seen rising ground to the north, crowned by a long belt of trees. This is Vicarwood, and the two mile ridgeway along the top is very pleasant, giving extensive views towards the city. This walk can be very muddy in wet weather so be well shod.

Leave the 'bus at Markeaton Lane on the Kedleston Road, and go along the lane and over Markeaton Brook to turn right within a short distance (car park nearly opposite). Continue past Stones Farm (formally Markeaton Stones) along a wide green lane. The lane becomes a cart track, passing through a gate to cross open fields. The spire of Quarndon Church comes into view and also a glimpse of Vicarwood, both seen from this valley of Markeaton Brook, lush with corn in the summer. The track makes a 'T' junction with a good farm road.

Turn left, climbing the open road through ploughed fields towards the trees on the hill-top. This is Vicarwood, once a fine belt of beeches but now thinned out with age and the elements. Ignoring a fork to the left, continue forward to Upper Vicarwood Farm, passing through the farmyard and leaving it through a white gate between a farm building and a row of poplar trees on the left. From here the ridgeway is a rough cart-track, very muddy in wet weather, and running beside now mixed woodland. On the far side of the wood is Kedleston Hall nestling in the valley, but ramblers do not trespass by leaving the track. To the south the open fields stretch down into the valleys of the Markeaton and Mackworth Brooks. Here is peace, quietness, perhaps broken only by the startling clatter of a pheasant.

The track comes out on the Kirk Langley-Kedleston lane opposite Priestwood Farm. Turn left to a lodge of Meynell Langley, where the gardens are open for the sale of garden plants etc. Pass through a wide gap on the left of the lodge entrance and continue along the hedge side bordering the gardens. Where they finish, go through an opening into the next field to continue straight ahead down the side of the hedges for two fields into the valley bottom.

Over a stile here, cross the middle of the field towards the left of the farm seen across the valley, when stiles will be found curving towards the farm. Mackworth Brook is crossed, and from here head up the middle of the field towards the top corner, and then towards a gate seen in a corner to the left of the farm. Step over a fence stile here, cross the field to the right of two gates, continuing down the hedge side on our left to pass to the right of a new house and join Ashbourne Road.

Turn left to Mackworth Village (about half a mile) and leave the main road by turning left down Jarvey's Lane to continue past the castle. Mackworth Castle is today but a gateway, all that is left of the home of the Mackworth family and which was built about 1500. Nevertheless it is impressive, and together with a neat row of cottages makes a pretty scene.